MP5124

PASSPORT SERIES
Australia, Oceania and Antarctica

Author: Heather Knowles
Contributors: Nancy Klepper (Australia)
Editor: Bonnie Krueger
Original Illustrations: Larry Nolte
Design and Layout: Kati Baker

Copyright: 2011 Lorenz Educational Press, a Lorenz company, and its licensors.
All rights reserved.

Permission to photocopy the student activities in this book is hereby granted to one teacher as part of the purchase price. This permission may only be used to provide copies for this teacher's specific classroom setting. This permission may not be transferred, sold, or given to any additional or subsequent user of this product. Thank you for respecting copyright laws.

Printed in the United States of America

ISBN 978-1-4291-2250-4

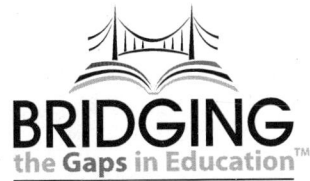

BRIDGING the Gaps in Education™
Lorenz Educational Press
P.O. Box 802 • Dayton, OH 45401-0802
for other LEP products visit our website
www.LorenzEducationalPress.com

*All statistics are based on information from 2010.
** For further information on pronunciations, research foreign language dictionaries and/or the Internet.

Metric Conversions

The purpose of this page is to aid in the conversion of measurements in this book from the English system to the metric system. Note that the tables below show two types of ounces. Liquid ounces measure the volume of liquids and have therefore been converted into milliliters. Dry ounces measure weight and have been converted into grams. Because dry substances such as sugar and flour may have different densities, it is advisable to measure them according to weight rather than volume. The measurement unit of the cup has been reserved solely for liquid, or volume, conversions.

Conversion Formulas

when you know	formula	to find / when you know	formula	to find
teaspoons	× 5	milliliters	× .20	teaspoons
tablespoons	× 15	milliliters	× .60	tablespoons
fluid ounces	× 29.57	milliliters	× .03	fluid ounces
liquid cups	× 240	milliliters	× .004	liquid cups
U.S. gallons	× 3.78	liters	× .26	U.S. gallons
dry ounces	× 28.35	grams	× .035	dry ounces
inches	× 2.54	centimeters	× .39	inches
square inches	× 6.45	square centimeters	× .15	square inches
feet	× .30	meters	× 3.28	feet
square feet	× .09	square meters	× 10.76	square feet
yards	× .91	meters	× 1.09	yards
miles	× 1.61	kilometers	× .62	miles
square miles	× 2.59	square kilometers	× .40	square miles
Fahrenheit	(°F − 32) × 5/9	Celsius	(°C × 9/5) + 32	Fahrenheit

Equivalent Temperatures
32°F = 0°C (water freezes)
212°F = 100°C (water boils)
350°F = 177°C
375°F = 191°C
400°F = 204°C
425°F = 218°C
450°F = 232°C

Common Cooking Conversions
1/2 cup = 120 milliliters
12 fluid ounces = 354.88 milliliters
1 quart (32 ounces) = 950 milliliters
1/2 gallon = 1.89 liters
1 Canadian gallon = 4.55 liters
8 dry ounces (1/2 pound) = 227 grams
16 dry ounces (1 pound) = 454 grams

Table of Contents

Australia 4

New Zealand 19

Papua New Guinea 32

Fiji 43

Antarctica 56

Answer Key 64

Additional Resources 65

Notes 66

Australia

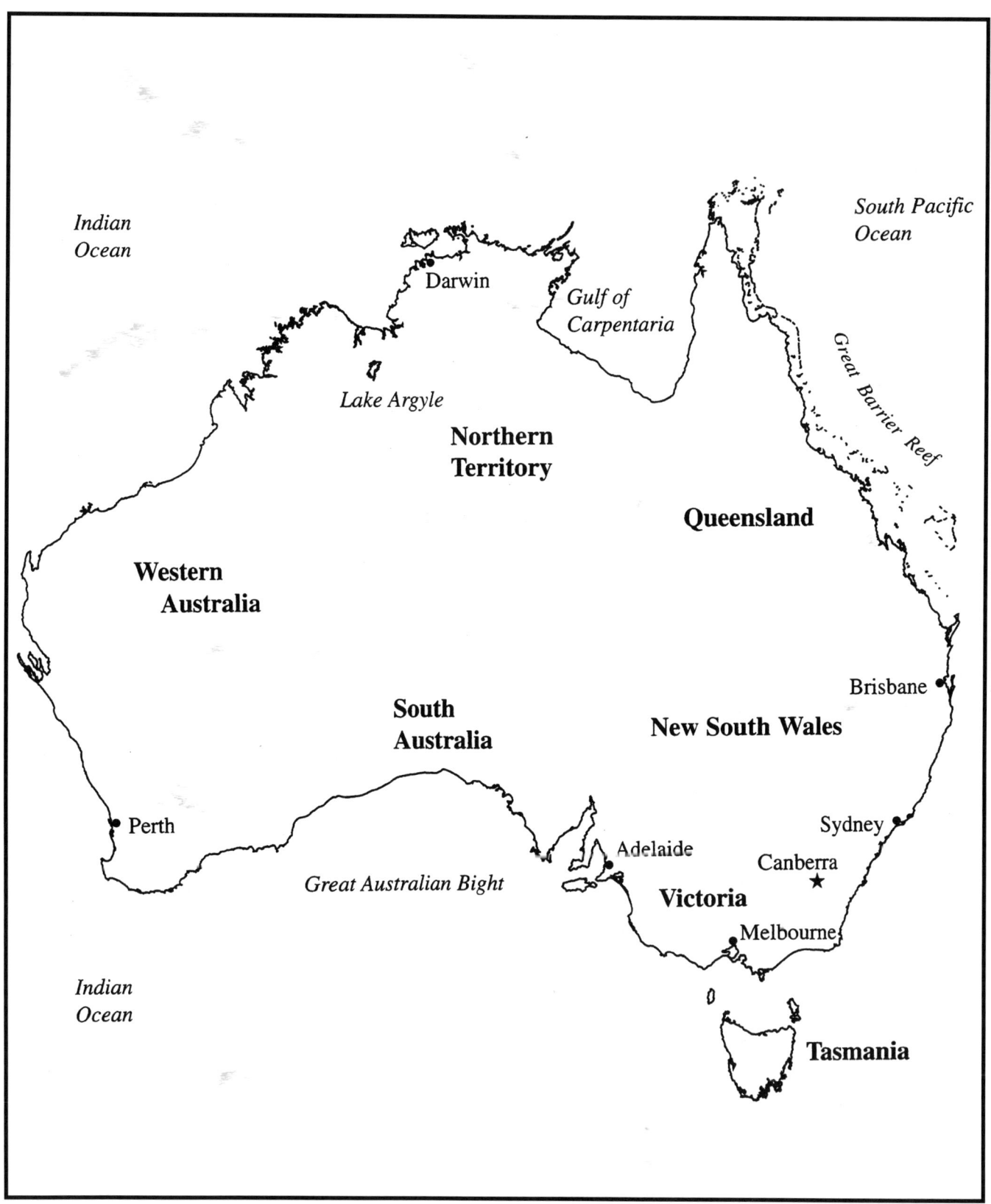

4

Australia - MP5124

Welcome to Australia!

The first Australians were the *Aborigines* (first settlers) who came to this island continent many thousands of years ago. The European settlement of Australia was established over 200 years ago, primarily by the British. Australia is similar to many European cultures, but due to its remote geographical location, it is sufficiently different to be considered another culture—a culture to which children can readily relate.

FAST FACTS

Official Name: Commonwealth of Australia

Location: Oceania, between the Indian Ocean and the South Pacific Ocean

Population: 21,515,754 (2010 estimate)

Capital City: Canberra

Area: 2,967,741 square miles; Australia is the sixth largest country in the world.

Major Language: English is the most widely spoken and is the official language. Aborigines have their own languages. People in the many immigrant communities also speak their native languages, such as Italian, Greek, and Vietnamese. 90 different languages are heard in Australia today.

Major Religion: Australia is predominately Christian, but a variety of other religions were brought to Australia by the diverse peoples who migrated there. Approximately 80 different religious groups exist in the country.

Currency: The Australian dollar   1 Australian dollar = 100 cents

Climate: Generally arid to semiarid; temperate in south and east; tropical in north

The Land: Mostly low plateau with deserts; fertile plain in southeast

Type of Government: Federal parliamentary democracy and a Commonwealth realm

Flag: The Australian flag is blue, with the flag of the United Kingdom in the upper hoist-side quadrant and a large seven-pointed star in the lower hoist-side quadrant. The star, known as the Commonwealth or Federation Star, represents the federation of the colonies of Australia in 1901. It depicts one point for each of the six original states and one representing all of Australia's internal and external territories. On the fly half of the flag is a representation of the Southern Cross constellation in white, with one small five-pointed star and four larger, seven-pointed stars.

Coat of Arms: In the center of the Australian coat of arms is a shield containing the badge of each Australian state. In the top half, from left to right, the states represented are New South Wales, Victoria, and Queensland, and in the bottom half, South Australia, Western Australia, and Tasmania. Above the shield is the seven-pointed Commonwealth Star above a blue and gold wreath. Six of the points on the star represent the original six states, while the seventh point represents the combined territories and any future states of Australia. The red kangaroo and emu, both native to Australia, are the unofficial animal emblems of the country.

National Flower: Golden wattle

National Animals: Kangaroo and emu (unofficial)

Natural Environment

Australia is unique in many ways. It is the only country that occupies an entire continent. The country is completely surrounded by water and could be considered the world's largest island. In fact, Australia is referred to as the "Island Continent." The land masses of Australia and Antarctica were once connected as indicated by the common fossil records of both continents. Australia is an old land; it is heavily eroded and has no significant mountains.

Australia is located in the Southern Hemisphere. Therefore, the stars in the night sky appear in different positions than the stars seen in North America. Some stars seen in North America can't be seen in Australia, such as Polaris, the North Star. Some stars seen in Australia can't be seen in North America, such as those found in a constellation called the Southern Cross, which has been incorporated into the design of the Australian flag.

Australia's location in the Southern Hemisphere also has an effect on the seasons. While countries in the Northern Hemisphere are experiencing winter, Australia is experiencing its summer; thus, Christmas in Australia is in the middle of summer. The Australian winter months are June, July, and August.

While the southern part of Australia has a temperate climate with distinct winters and summers, the northern part of Australia is semitropical or tropical, like the Caribbean. Much of the Australian interior is desert or semi-arid. The largest reef in the world, the Great Barrier Reef, stretches more than 1,500 miles along the northeast coast of Australia.

Australia is on the east side of the International Date Line that stretches from north to south across the Pacific Ocean. Sydney and Melbourne, the two largest cities in Australia, are about 15 hours ahead of Toronto, making Australia almost a day ahead of North American countries. When travelers go from North America to Australia, they lose a day as they cross the International Date Line. Of course, they gain a day when they return.

Australia is sometimes referred to as being "down under," which means that it is below Europe and North America. Of course the earth is round and can be viewed from any perspective. Europeans historically thought of themselves as being "on top." So when they drew maps of the world they put Europe at the top of the map and Africa, South America, and Australia at the bottom of the map.

Animal and Plant Life

Because Australia has been separated from other lands for millions of years, its plants and animals have evolved differently from plants and animals elsewhere on the earth. As a result, Australia has several unique species of plants and animals.

Kangaroo

The *marsupials*, the most familiar of these unique species, have 170 subspecies. Marsupials keep their newborns in a pouch on the mother's body until they are old enough to care for themselves. Kangaroos, wallabies, and koalas are the best-known marsupials.

Kookaburra

Australia has the only egg-laying mammals—the duck-billed platypus and the *echidna*, or spiny anteater! They belong to a group called *monotremes*, which lay eggs covered with soft, leathery shells like those of reptiles.

Australia also has birds found nowhere else in the world, such as the emu, lyrebird, and bowerbird. The best known Australian bird is the kookaburra, famous for its call that fills the air with a sound like laughter.

Almost 24,000 plants are unique to this continent. Unfortunately, many of Australia's plants and animals have become extinct since the arrival of the first European settlers. The Australian government now places a high priority on the conservation of this land's unique natural resources. Government rangers and scientists are working together to keep Australia's plants and animals safe. School children and adults join the Australian Trust for Conservation Volunteers and work to protect the natural environment. They plant trees and build fences to protect wildlife.

In Your Classroom

Bring a world map and a globe to the classroom and let the children explore them. Introduce basic geographical concepts—equator, Northern and Southern Hemispheres, International Date Line, oceans, and landforms. Try putting south at the top and viewing the world from this perspective.

Discuss the issue of extinct and endangered species. *World* magazine from the National Geographic Society and *Ranger Rick* and *Your Big Backyard* magazines from the National Wildlife Federation are good resources for this purpose. Let the children explore ways they can act to protect their environment.

A History of Australia

European Settlement

The first European explorers to reach Australia found it a strange and inhospitable land. Dutch and English seamen reported that there was little food, few trees, and no fresh water.

On a later expedition, Captain James Cook claimed Australia as a British colony. Not many people wanted to go to Australia, so the British decided to settle the new colony by sending criminals as punishment for crimes committed in Britain. Others were sent to Australia for disagreeing with British colonial rule. A convict's family often came along to settle in this new country.

Captain James Cook

Britain stopped sending convicts to Australia in the 19th century. Convicts who served their time were freed and, in most cases, became honest citizens. Britain encouraged other people to migrate from Britain, and many came, especially from Ireland and England. Today, people from all parts of Europe, South and North America, Asia, and the Middle East live in Australia.

The population of Australia grew substantially during several gold rushes in the 19th century. An Australian miner who had gone to California to search for gold returned to Australia and found gold in rock similar to the gold-bearing geological formations of California. The rush was on, and cities emptied as men rushed to the newly discovered gold fields. Some of the gold miners, known as *diggers*, made fortunes, but many did not. The gold-mining frenzy in Australia was a time of glamour and excitement.

Britain formed six separate colonies on the Australian continent, each with its own English governor. But by 1880, the colonies recognized the need to work together. The six Australian colonies formed a federation when they became independent from Britain in 1906. Today, the Commonwealth of Australia has a parliamentary system of government modeled after the British parliament.

Aborigines, Australia's First People

Before Europeans arrived, Australia was believed by many to be "terra nullis," a land belonging to no one. This was not true. Aborigines are the oldest inhabitants of Australia. They have lived there for at least 47,000 years—maybe longer.

More than 200 years ago, at the time of European settlement, there were hundreds of different Aboriginal groups living throughout Australia. They didn't think of Australia as one country, but as many separate places where each group belonged. Aborigines lived with the land in a way that was not comprehensible to the first Europeans.

Aborigines knew the rhythm of nature and the changing weather cycles. They knew where to find certain plants and where to dig roots. They knew when and where to catch animals and fish, where to trap birds, and where to collect eggs. They were highly skilled hunters and gatherers, living where Europeans would have perished.

Aborigines were also skilled tool makers, and they fashioned boomerangs, spears, clubs, nets, traps, stone axes, and fire sticks from natural materials. They believed that the symbols used to decorate their implements were sacred and gave them strength from the world of spirits. Thus, a boomerang decorated with wavy lines or herringbone patterns would always fly true when thrown at prey. In this way, the Aborigines combined religion with economics and art.

European settlers did not understand or respect the patterns of Aboriginal life. They took the land for their own and fenced it in for cattle and sheep. Their livestock trampled plants, competed with wild animals for food, and muddied the water holes.

Aborigines tried to continue their traditional way of life, but they were driven off many lands by Europeans. Aborigines were hunted and poisoned, and many died. Originally, there were about 300,000 Aborigines; today there are about 50,000 full-blooded Aborigines.

Daily Life

In many ways, life in Australia is similar to life in any European culture, but there are differences. Vast areas of the interior of Australia are desert, and other areas are semiarid. As a result, most of Australia's population lives near the more hospitable coasts. In Australia's large cities—Sydney, Melbourne, Brisbane, Adelaide, Hobart, and Perth—people live much as they do in cities all over North America and Europe.

Australia is one of the most urban countries in the world, but its rural history shapes the way Australians and the rest of the world view the country. In the sparsely settled countryside, which Australians refer to as the *outback,* or *bush,* some people live on large cattle and sheep ranches called *stations*. Stations are very far apart and are usually located hundreds of miles from any city. The distances are so great between neighbors that families communicate by two-way radio networks. Isolation forces families living on stations to be self-reliant. Families must even provide for their own medical care.

Each station has a complete medical kit in case of injury or sickness. Medical advice can be obtained over the radio. If help is needed, a mobile medical service can be contacted by radio so that personnel can then be flown to the station, and if necessary, the sick or injured person can be flown out to an urban hospital.

Some children on stations have no nearby schools to attend. Since commuting such long distances is impractical, these children must take lessons by two-way radio from a *School of the Air*. Along with lessons in math, reading, and history, children share events, sing songs, have parties and interact with friends—all by radio!

In Your Classroom

Pretend that children are living in the outback and have to attend a School of the Air. Set up a radio classroom with toy walkie-talkies. Children take turns being "teacher."

Language & Expressions

Due to the ancestry of its people, many Australian expressions are British in origin. There are many uniquely Australian expressions as well.

g'day – good day
cobber – friend, workmate
mate – friend
digger – originally a goldminer, now a soldier
dinkum – true, honest; "fair dinkum" means quite true, genuine
good on you – general term of approval
ta – farewell, goodbye
mum – mother
ripper – good, great, as in "what a ripper"
beaut – nice, good, as in "you did a beaut job"
nick off – get lost
barbie – a barbecue
okie dokie – OK
tucker – food
tea – dinner

Myths

Aboriginal culture has many myths and legends about the earth's origins. Before Europeans arrived in Australia, Aborigines had no written language, and all myths and legends were handed down by word of mouth. Aboriginal myths express the ancient origins of life and the land which, according to their beliefs, began long ago in the "Dreamtime." In this distant time, creatures resembling human beings rose out of the featureless plains where they had been sleeping for countless ages. They started to wander about the countryside. As they wandered, they carried out everyday tasks—they hunted, dug for water, made fires, camped, and performed ceremonies.

Then the Dreamtime suddenly ended, and wherever these beings had been active, some natural feature was created. Thus mountains, rivers, valleys, and hills represent events from the Dreamtime. These creatures are also responsible for the existence of all animals and plants, as well as the creation of fire for cooking and warmth, wooden bowls, the first tools, and the laws that govern all aspects of life, relationships, and ceremonies.

In ancient times, myths were accepted by Aborigines as both the absolute truth and the answer to all of life's questions. The myths embodied the Aboriginal philosophy of life and were the basis for all art, music, and ceremonial life. As Greek myths have contributed greatly to western art, Aboriginal myths have contributed greatly to Australian art and society.

How the Kangaroos Got Their Tails
In the early days of the Dreamtime, there were two kangaroos. The plains kangaroo was big and had long arms and legs. The hill kangaroo was small and had short arms and legs.

One day, the short kangaroo found some sugarbag in a hole in the rock. He reached just inside the hole and pulled out a handful. Mmmm. It was good tucker.

Now the big kangaroo was pretty hungry for sugarbag too. "Reach right in and get some," said the short kangaroo. So the big kangaroo put his long arm deep into the hole and pulled out a handful of spiders! UGH! He tried again but pulled out more and more spiders. The short kangaroo kept reaching just inside the hole and pretty soon he had eaten all the sugarbag.

The big kangaroo went wild and started a fight. He threw a stick and it stuck in the back of the short kangaroo. The short kangaroo threw a stick and it stuck in the back of the big kangaroo. They both left for their own countries forever. When you see them, you will know how they got their tails.

The Myth of the First Kangaroo
The first kangaroos were blown to Australia by a violent windstorm. The wind blew them along on their journey and they were so exhausted that they could not land, so their hind legs grew longer and longer as they tried to touch the ground.

A party of Aborigines was hunting when the windstorm struck. The storm drove them into the shelter of some nearby rocks. As they looked up into the clouds, they saw the kangaroos being carried along by the wind. They had never seen such strange animals, with their small heads and front legs, and their large bodies, tails, and hind legs.

During a lull in the storm, the hunters saw one kangaroo become lodged in a tree, fall to the ground, and hop away. An animal that large would provide food for many people, so the whole tribe moved to the area where the kangaroo had been seen. It was a good place with lots of flowing water, fruit trees, and grass. It was a long time, however, before Aborigines learned how to hunt the kangaroo, the largest and swiftest of all the Australian animals.

The Myth of Tiddalik, the Flood-Maker
Tiddalik, the largest frog in the world, awoke one morning with a terrible thirst. He started to drink. He drank and he drank and he drank until there was no water left in the world. He had drunk it all.

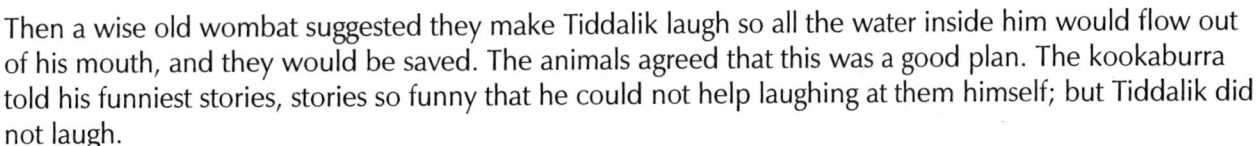

The animals of the world started to die, and the plants started to shrivel because there was no water. The animals gathered together and talked about their terrible fate. They didn't know what to do.

Then a wise old wombat suggested they make Tiddalik laugh so all the water inside him would flow out of his mouth, and they would be saved. The animals agreed that this was a good plan. The kookaburra told his funniest stories, stories so funny that he could not help laughing at them himself; but Tiddalik did not laugh.

The kangaroo jumped over the emu, and the blanket lizard waddled up and down on two legs making his stomach stick out. Tiddalik's face did not change, and he did not laugh.

The animals were very disappointed and about to despair when the eel, Nabunum, came slithering up. He had been driven from his favorite creek by the drought. He began to dance, slowly at first with graceful movements. Then faster and faster he danced, and he wriggled and twisted himself into the most comical shapes. Suddenly Tiddalik's eyes lit up, and he burst out laughing.

As he laughed, the water gushed out of his mouth, and the rivers, streams, lakes, and swamps were filled with water once more. All of the animals and plants were saved.

Famous Australian Proverbs

Here are some famous Australian proverbs. What do you think they mean?

Those who lose dreaming are lost.

Keep your eyes on the sun and you will not see the shadows.

The more you know, the less you need.

In Your Classroom

Invite an Australian to visit the class and to tell students about Australia. Ask students to listen for differences between Australian speech and their own dialect.

Students can compose dramas based on Aboriginal myths.

Invite students to create their own myths and act them out.

Play "telephone." Invite students to sit in a circle. Select one person to make up a message or riddle. Pass the message on to the next student who passes the message to the next child, and so on. The last person in the circle tells the message aloud. Is it different from the original message? Discuss how stories and legends can change when they are passed on by word of mouth.

Make cat's cradles. Aborigines made string out of bark-fiber, and from the string, they made over 400 cat's-cradle designs. These designs were used as games and storytelling aids. Use twine and practice some cat's-cradle patterns. Ask students to talk about the cat's-cradle designs and discuss what they portray. Create stories related to the cat's cradle.

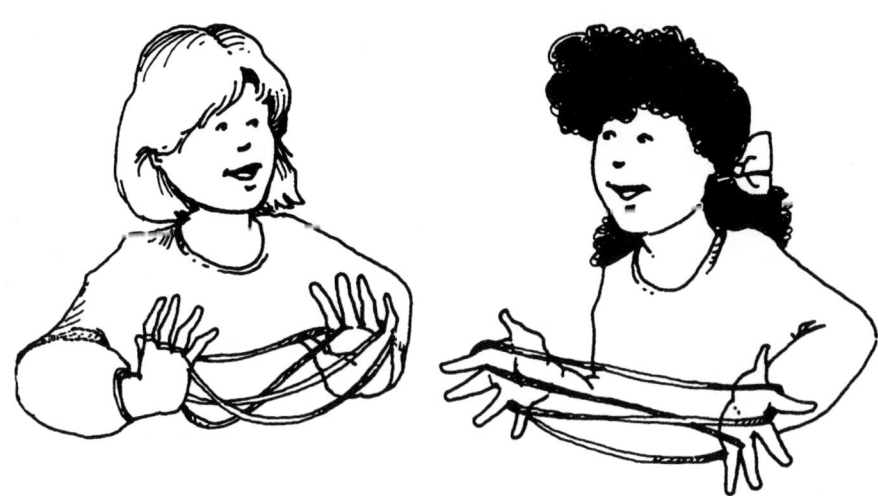

Australian English

In talking to an Australian, you may hear some words and phrases that are a bit unfamiliar to you. Since early Australian settlers were from Great Britain, many uniquely English phrases crept into the Australian vocabulary. Also, Australians love to abbreviate words—just like their English ancestors. See if you can match the terms in the left-hand column to their meaning in Australian English on the right.

1. _____ ketchup   a. biscuit
2. _____ good   b. ta
3. _____ cookie   c. mum
4. _____ broken   d. barbie
5. _____ French fries   e. tucker
6. _____ dinner   f. chokkie
7. _____ goodbye   g. bunged up
8. _____ root beer   h. cobber
9. _____ friend   i. tomato sauce
10. _____ mother   j. sasprillla
11. _____ soldier   k. digger
12. _____ barbeque   l. prezzy
13. _____ a present or gift   m. tea
14. _____ food   n. chips
15. _____ chocolate   o. ripper

FOODS

Australian food is very similar to food found in North America and Great Britain, but with a few interesting differences. Tea is a very important drink in Australia and a glass of tea is referred to as a *cuppa*. Breakfast is a big meal, and lunch is traditionally lighter. Dinner is called *tea!*

Australians like hamburgers and hot dogs, but they also like *Vegemite sandwiches, creme buns, pies, pasties, sausage rolls, Anzac biscuits, minties,* and *pumpkin scones.*

- *Vegemite* is a salty vegetable and yeast spread, used like peanut butter
- *Creme buns* are pastries filled with whipped cream.
- *Pies* and *pasties* are pastries filled with cooked meat or potatoes.
- *Anzac biscuits* are cookies. (See recipe on page 28.)
- *Minties* are candies.
- *Pumpkin scones* are pumpkin pastries.

Scones

Hundreds and Thousands Sandwiches
To make these simple sandwiches, spread margarine on whole wheat bread and cover generously with colored sprinkles. This is a fun snack that children can easily make by themselves.

Pikelets
Pikelets are similar to pancakes, but they are smaller, and they make delicious and nutritious snacks.

½ cup whole wheat flour
½ cup white flour
1 tbsp baking powder
1 ripe banana, mashed
1 tsp grated lemon rind
squeeze of lemon juice
enough milk to make a consistent, dropping batter

Combine dry ingredients, and then stir in banana and milk, preferably low-fat milk. Drop spoonfuls of mixture onto a heated, lightly greased, nonstick skillet. As bubbles appear on top of each pikelet, turn over so the other side browns. Remove from pan and serve topped with slices of fresh banana. Recipe makes 12 pikelets.

Icypoles (Popsicles)
Mix equal amounts of unsweetened apple juice, orange juice, and unsweetened pineapple juice in a large container. Freeze in molds.

For a creamier-textured icypole, blend chopped fresh fruits with an equal amount of nonfat yogurt and freeze in molds or ice cube trays.

Queensland Sunshine Coast Fruit Salad
Gather equal quantities of banana chunks, apple chunks, orange segments, strawberries, pineapple chunks and kiwi fruit, and lemon juice to taste.

Squeeze lemon juice over banana and apple. Combine all the fruit and toss lightly. Chill well before serving.

In Your Classroom

Make Australian treats to serve at snack time. Compare Australian foods with foods eaten in your region.

Holidays & Festivals

As a primarily European culture, the Australians celebrate many of the same religious and secular holidays celebrated throughout the West. The following are celebrations that are unique to Australia.

Australia Day • *January 26*
Australia celebrates what's great about the country and what could be done to make it even better on this biggest holiday honoring the founding of the first settlement in Australia. The sunny summer weather makes it easy for Australians to gather throughout the country for concerts, barbeques, ceremonies, or a day at the beach.

Harmony Day • *March 21*
This day celebrates Australians' respect for community harmony and cultural diversity. Local communities put on special events that highlight understanding and respect. In past years, some Harmony Day student activities have included releasing balloons with messages of hope, creating a school jigsaw puzzle with each student contributing a piece, and designing postcards with a harmony theme.

Melbourne Cup Day • *First Tuesday of November*
This is Australia's most famous Tuesday of the year. Everyone tunes their TVs to the Melbourne Cup, a world-famous horse race. Those in Melbourne get the day off. Those in other places have a party to celebrate. Those lucky enough to attend the actual race make a day —and a fashion show—of it by wearing their best clothes and, for the ladies, big hats!

The Great Australian Barbie
During the Australian summer, barbecues are very popular at home and at the beach. Australians barbecue every imaginable kind of meat, including lamb and fish. Families celebrate and friends gather to play games, to sing songs, to dance, and to eat.

Surf Carnival
Much of Australia's population lives within a few miles of an ocean beach. The beaches are patrolled by surf lifesaving clubs made up of volunteers. The lifeguards rescue many surfers and swimmers each year. The lifeguard associations compete in surf lifesaving drills, a unique Australian sport. The competitions include swimming, simulated lifesaving, and marching drills. Each lifesaving team has its own uniform and banner. The banners are elaborate and proudly displayed.

In Your Classroom

Have a *barbie* (barbecue). Students may dress as *diggers* (gold miners) and *swagmen* (hobos). Diggers wear jeans, miners' shirts, and boots. Swagmen wear jeans, vests, a kerchief around the neck, and wide-brimmed hats with corks hanging from strings tied to the brim (to keep the Australian bush flies away).

Grill *rissoles* (hamburgers) and *snags* (sausages or hot dogs) served with lots of *tom sauce* (ketchup). Also serve coleslaw, Queensland Sunshine Coast fruit salad, and Anzac biscuits (see recipes on page 28).

Have a surf carnival around wading pools set up in the playground. Play water games. Serve icypoles and hundreds and thousands sandwiches.

Invite a lifeguard or swimming instructor to the surf carnival. Talk about water safety.

Invite other classrooms to the surf carnival. Have each class make a water-safety banner from a sheet or large piece of paper. Hang the banners at the carnival.

MP5124 - Australia

Creative Arts

Music, Dance, Arts

Songs
Everyone likes to sing, and Australia has many songs of its own. The following song is known the world over:

"Once a jolly swagman camped by a billabong,
Under the shade of a coolibah tree;
And he sang as he watched and waited till his billy boiled,
'You'll come a-waltzing Matilda with me!'"

Waltzing Matilda is the most famous Australian song, but few people outside Australia understand what it means. *Swagman* is an Australian word for *hobo*. *Matilda* is the hobo's bedroll or blanket that is rolled up and slung across his shoulder when walking. A *billabong* is a pond or small body of water. A *billy* is a small pail used to cook and to heat water for tea.

Painting
In traditional Aboriginal society, art served a ritual function. Paintings on bark, wood, engraved rocks, decorated tools, and even humans all related to Aboriginal beliefs about the origins of the earth and its relationship to the spirits that created it.

Aboriginal painting is distinctive and highly original. Images include Australian animals such as kangaroos, snakes, and lizards, as well as geometric shapes. Aborigines were very knowledgable about the anatomy of Australian animals, and they often created "x-ray pictures," showing the animal's internal organs. Aborigines used the colors of nature—red for the color of clay, white for the fire ashes, black for charcoal, and brown and ocher for the earth. Paintings were made on bark, wood, stone, and on the human body. The artist believed the act of painting, the giving of his own energy, was more important than the painting itself.

Dance
Aborigines believe that their chants, songs, and dances were given to them by the spirits. Some chants are so old that meanings have been lost as Aboriginal languages have changed. Dance symbolizes everyday events from nature. Dancers mimic the movements of birds, fish, and other animals, as well as storms and the sea.

Aboriginals dance for entertainment and for sacred ritual observances. Dancing for entertainment expresses joy and happiness at events like weddings and successful hunts. The steps are mostly basic—a skip, a shuffle, a stamp—but always exuberant!

Sacred dances recreate myths and are part of initiation ceremonies and rituals such as ones to ensure adequate food supplies. Sacred dances are only taught to and performed for those who have been initiated.

Dances are performed to chanting, singing, the clapping of hands, dance sticks and boomerangs, and the playing of flutes. A singing and dancing gathering is called a *corroboree*. Its purpose was to persuade the ancestors and spirits to help with everyday life—in the initiation of youth into adulthood, in the success of a hunt, and in the joy of entertainment.

In Your Classroom

Read the book, *Waltzing Matilda*, by Andrew Peterson (New York: HarperCollins, 1991). Learn the song and make some "billy tea" by boiling loose herbal tea in a pot (strain before serving). A recording of the song can be found at most libraries.

Aborigines made message sticks, or small, carved wood tablets, as invitations to ceremonies and hunts, as "shopping lists," and as IOUs. Make message sticks in class. Ask students to create a code. Using strips of plywood or thick cardboard, write coded messages on the wood and send them to classmates to decode.

Aborigines painted necklaces with geometric shapes. Using cardboard or dried clay disks with a small hole at the top, paint assorted geometric shapes and string the necklaces with yarn.

Aboriginal families or clans each have a special plant, animal, or natural sign called a totem that identifies its members with the group. Ask students to choose an animal or creature to become the class totem. Draw pictures of the totem to display.

Hold a corroboree.

Make an Australian flute (*didjeridoo*) from a cardboard cylinder or a hollow piece of wood or bamboo 4 to 5 feet long and about two inches across. Play the didjeridoo by blowing across one end.

Make rhythm sticks out of dowel sticks or paper cylinders and decorate them with Aboriginal signs.

Tell Aboriginal stories and then act out myths by dancing. Children can mimic Australian animals, like the kangaroo, and natural phenomena, like rain or a flowing river. Be sure to stamp and move the feet. Do the dance slowly at first, and then repeat it at a faster tempo.

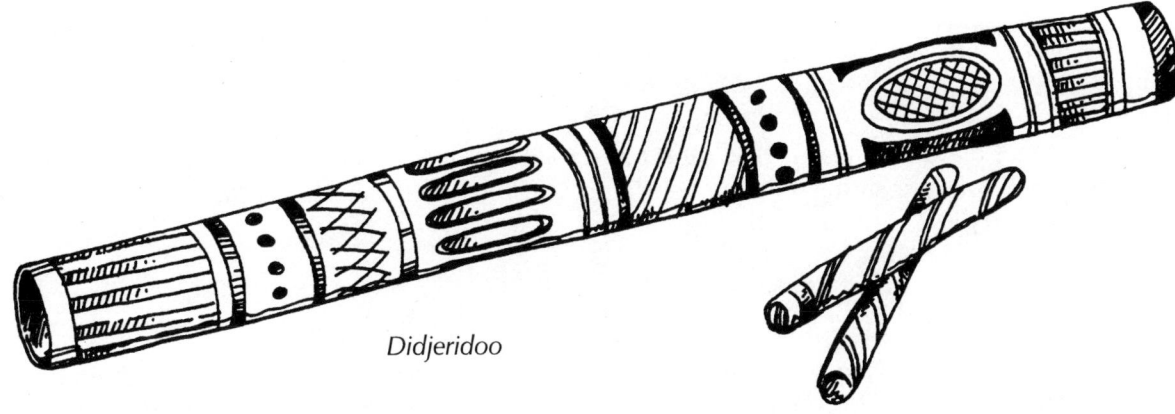

Didjeridoo

MP5124 - Australia

Sports & Games

Australians love sports and outdoor activities, and the country's warm climate makes it easy to participate in both. Cricket (similar to American baseball), rugby, soccer, cycling, rowing, competitive boat racing, swimming, track and field, field hockey, tennis, horse racing, and motor racing—whether people participate in them or watch them on TV—are among the most popular sports. Netball, a game similar to basketball, is the most popular team sport for women. And at any international sporting event you will hear the crowd roar *"Aussie! Aussie! Aussie!"* when rooting for their teams.

Cricket

Games
Children the world over create games, and Australian children are no exception. Many Australian children's rhymes have been handed down from generation to generation.

Jump Rope Chants
Koala bear, koala bear, touch the ground,
Koala bear, koala bear, turn around,
Koala bear, koala bear, climb up the stairs,
Koala bear, koala bear, say your prayers,
Koala bear, koala bear, switch off the light,
Koala bear, koala bear, say good night.

See you later alligator, In a while crocodile, Not tonight vegemite, Oo roo, kangaroo.

Bowls
Bowls is a popular game played on a lawn. The object is to roll large, black balls as close as possible to a small, white ball, called a jack, which is sitting on the other side of the lawn. The balls that come closest to the jack without touching, win. Try it!

In Your Classroom

Ask students to gather their own collection of rhymes, games, jokes, riddles, and tall tales. Write them down or ask the children to dictate them into an audio recorder. Invite parents to the class and have them talk about rhymes and games they played when they were children. Play some of these games during free time.

Most schools in Australia have sports days each year. Hold a sports day for your class. Invite other rooms to join. Play field games, including races and relays, with partners or alone. Hold ball-throwing contests. Everyone gets a ribbon!

If there is a cricket association in your community, invite a member to come to your class with cricket equipment and to tell students about the game.

New Zealand

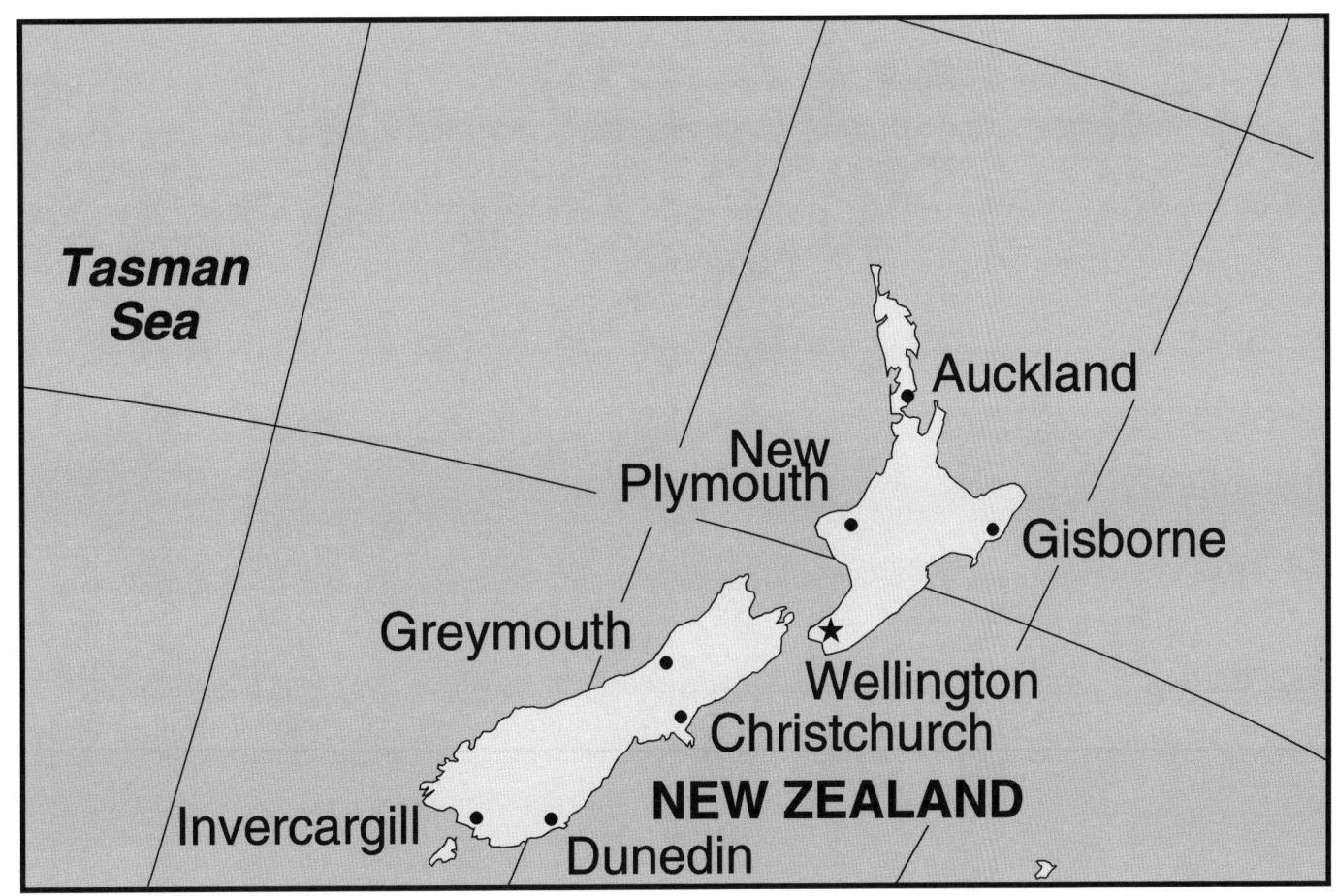

Welcome to New Zealand!

New Zealand is an isolated island in the South Pacific. The island is over 1,000 miles southeast of Australia, its closest neighbor. New Zealand is very long and slightly larger than the United Kingdom. The country is known for its beautiful scenery and unique wildlife.

Official Name:	New Zealand
Location:	Oceania, southeast of Australia
Population:	4,252,277 (2010 estimate)
Capital City:	Wellington
Area:	100,000 square miles (268,000 square kilometers)
Major Language:	Most New Zealanders speak English. About a third of the Maoris speak the Maori language and it is taught in many schools. The only other non-English language spoken on the island is Samoan.
Major Religion:	New Zealand has no state religion, but about three-fifths of the population is Christian. Anglican cathedrals are used for official or governmental occasions. The rest of the population is either not religious or has created its own adaptation of Christianity by combining its teachings with Maori beliefs.
Currency:	New Zealand dollar 1 New Zealand dollar = 100 cents
Climate:	Temperate with sharp regional contrasts
The Land:	Predominately mountainous with some large coastal plains
Type of Government:	Parliamentary democracy and a Commonwealth realm
Flag:	New Zealand's flag is deep blue, with the British Union flag in the upper left corner. In the center of the flag are four red stars from the Southern Cross constellation.

Coat of Arms:	In the center of the coat of arms is a shield divided into four quarters. The first quarter contains four stars representing the Southern Cross constellation, the second quarter shows a golden fleece (representing the agricultural industry), the third quarter has a wheat sheaf (also representing agriculture), and the fourth quarter shows two hammers (representing mining and industry). Down the center of the shield is a strip with three ships (representing the importance of sea trade). The shield is supported by a blonde woman of European descent holding the New Zealand flag and a Maori warrior holding a ceremonial spear. On top of the shield is the St Edward's Crown, and beneath it are two silver fern leaves and a scroll with the words "New Zealand".
National Flower:	Kowhai
National Animal:	Kiwi

Natural Environment

New Zealand is known as one of the most beautiful countries in the world. Its magnificent mountains, lush green valleys, and thundering rivers have been used in many films, including *Lord of the Rings*. Two-thirds of the country's land is able to be used for farming, and the other third is made up of mountains. Because it is an island, the country has many harbors and fjords. Nothing in New Zealand is more than 80 miles from the coast, and most places have gorgeous mountain views.

The Southern Alps are a 300-mile long chain of mountains. Mount Cook, the tallest mountain in New Zealand with an elevation of 12,316 feet, is located here. The country is also filled with numerous glaciers. The largest of these is called the Tasman Glacier and is 18 miles long and 1.5 miles wide.

Most of the population lives on the North Island. Auckland, the largest city, and Wellington, the capital, are both located there. The mountains of the North Island are less steep than in the south. North Island's climate is much milder, and its lower terrain gives it more economic potential. Most of the farmland is located in the west, especially the dairy farms, which produce important exports. The country is known for its volcanic activity. A large volcanic plateau is located in the center of the island, and the largest lake, Taupo, is formed by an ancient volcanic crater.

Other significant islands, Niue and Cook, are self-governing states in free association with New Zealand.

Because of New Zealand's latitude, isolation, and physical characteristics, the country does not experience extreme temperatures. It has a mild climate ranging between 50 and 70 degrees Fahrenheit year round. Usually, it snows on the mountains, but very rarely in the lowlands.

New Zealand has very diverse wildlife. Two-thirds of the island is covered with evergreen forests. Because of the country's long isolation from the rest of the world, about 90% of its plants are distinct only to New Zealand. Extremely dense parts of the forest, known as the *bush*, make some areas unsuitable for settling. Some of the bush has been made into parks or reserves. Because New Zealand has such an abundant amount of trees, it produces some of the best timber used in industry. Erosion is a problem in some parts of the highlands, however, due to European settlement.

When the Europeans came to New Zealand, they brought with them some species of animals, such as the red deer and Australian opossum. The island has no predatory animals, making it a paradise for flightless birds. The most famous flightless bird is the *kiwi*, which has become a nickname for New Zealanders. Tropical fish, seals, and dolphins can be found in the seas that surround the beautiful island.

New Zealand is filled with minerals, coal, iron, gold, natural gas, and construction materials. Hydroelectricity (or water power) supplies a large amount of the country's power. New Zealand farms raise livestock and sheep for grazing, and produce meat and dairy products such as cheese and milk. The country's economy is dependent on exporting agricultural products, especially to Great Britain. When the United Kingdom joined the European Community in the 1970s, New Zealand expanded its trade with other countries. In recent decades, pastoral farming has declined. Other industries have expanded throughout the country, such as forestry, fishing, deer farming, and manufacturing. The tourism industry is also important for New Zealand's economy. Visitors from all over the world go there to experience the relaxed culture and breathtaking scenery.

Kiwi

In Your Classroom

Have each student keep a New Zealand folder. Glue a piece of white paper on the front of the folder and have each student draw and color New Zealand's flag using paints, markers, colored pencils, or crayons. On the back of the folder, glue another piece of white paper and have students draw a map of New Zealand, labeling the capital and other large cities and bodies of water. Use these folders to hold papers and activities from the lesson.

Use a chart of the various constellations and point out the Southern Cross to the students. Then pass out the graphing activity on page 23. Explain why some constellations are only visible in the northern hemisphere and why others are only visible in the southern hemisphere. Plan a class stargazing trip, or assign students to find various constellations on their own.

Show a clip from *Lord of the Rings* to give the students an idea of the beautiful New Zealand landscape.

Bring in magazines with pictures of New Zealand. Have the students cut them out and paste them on pieces of paper. Hang these pieces of paper along the classroom wall to make a mural.

Assign each student a different species of New Zealand wildlife. Have each student sketch a picture of his or her animal. Hang the sketches around the room, and have students view them as if they were visiting an exhibit at the zoo.

Name _____ Date _____

The Night Sky

The Southern Cross constellation (also called *Crux*) is only one of many constellations in the night sky.

Plot the points on the graphs. Then write the name of the constellation shown on the line below each graph. Use the pictures at the bottom of the page to help you connect the stars!

1. (4, 1) (4, 7)
   (2, 4) (6, 5)

2. (6, 1) (0, 7) (3, 5)
   (2, 6) (7, 3)
   (4, 4) (4, 2)

3. (3, 2) (1, 1) (4, 4)
   (4, 7) (5, 0) (6, 6)
   (6, 8) (5, 6) (8, 5)

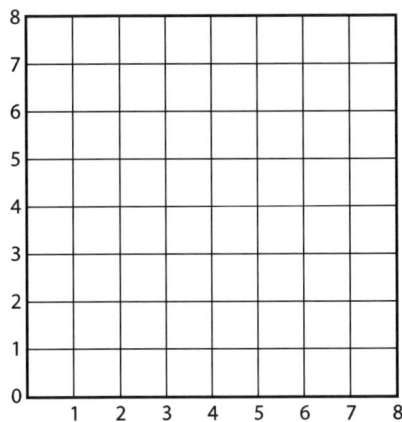
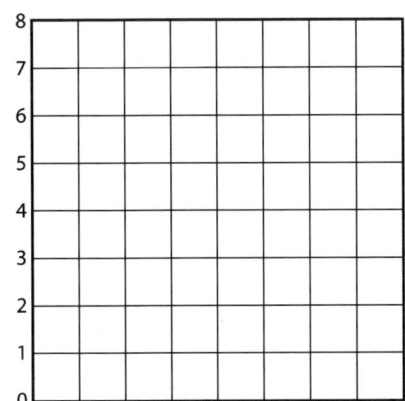
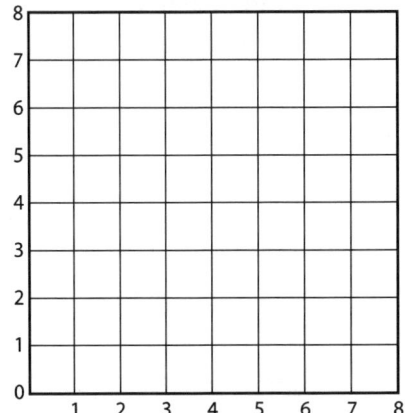

4. (3, 4) (4, 7) (1, 6) (5, 6)
   (7, 6) (4, 4) (2, 4)
   (1, 2) (5, 2) (7, 7)

5. (4, 3) (5, 4) (2, 6) (2, 1)
   (6, 8) (6, 6) (5, 8) (5, 0)
   (2, 5) (1, 6) (3, 0)

6. (2, 1) (5, 7) (3, 1) (5, 4)
   (0, 5) (6, 5) (6, 0) (6, 8)
   (3, 6) (8, 2) (7, 4) (3, 5)
   (2, 8) (4, 3)

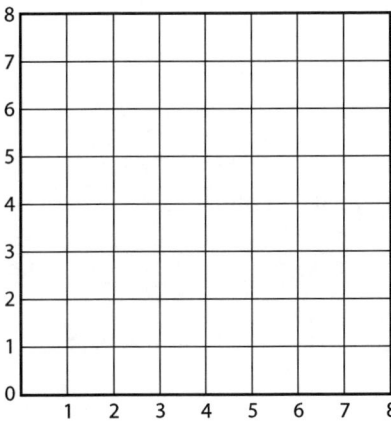
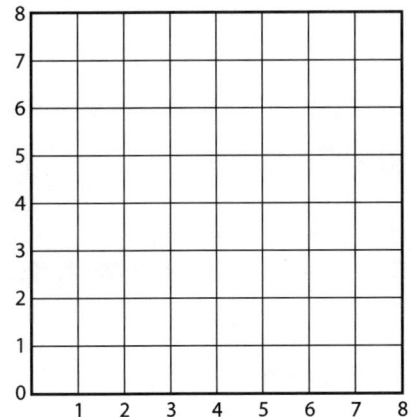
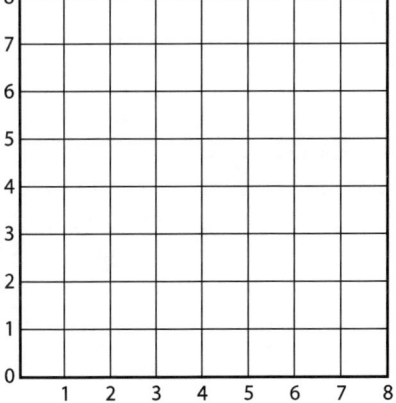

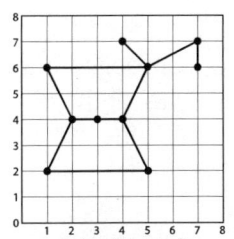
Orion (Hunter)   Canis Major (Big Dog)   Ursa Major (Big Dipper)   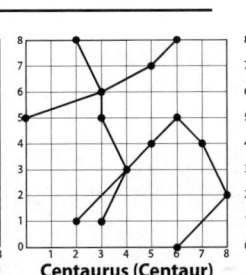 Centaurus (Centaur)   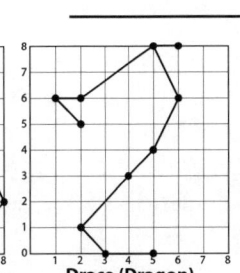 Draco (Dragon)   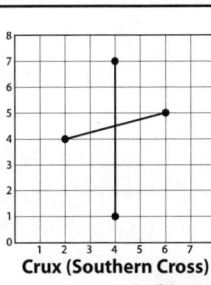 Crux (Southern Cross)

MP5124 - New Zealand

A History of New Zealand

Early New Zealand

New Zealand was isolated from the rest of the world for thousands of years. The country was first settled by Polynesians, now known as Maoris, over 1,000 years ago. These people came from the middle of the South Pacific and settled mostly on the North Island. When the Europeans began to arrive, the Polynesians called themselves *Maori* (which translates as "normal") to distinguish themselves from the Europeans.

Exploration

The first European explorer to arrive in New Zealand was a Dutchman named Abel Janszoon Tasman who came in 1642. It was British naval captain James Cook that visited the islands between 1769 and 1777 and gave them the name *New Zealand*. Europeans began to come regularly to New Zealand. Most of these immigrants were from Great Britain, and their numbers increased even more when New Zealand was annexed by the United Kingdom in 1840.

With them, Europeans brought diseases to which the Maoris had no resistance. Sadly, many of the Maoris died because of this. The Maoris and the Europeans fought each other frequently, and by 1896 only 42,000 Maoris were alive in New Zealand. In the early 20th century, the Maori population began to grow again. By this time they were having large families and had developed resistance to European diseases.

Many central Europeans migrated to New Zealand during the World Wars to escape the violence in their home countries. Asians also immigrated to New Zealand from China and India.

Independence

In 1947, New Zealand gained its independence from Britain and became an independent member of the Commonwealth of Nations. Today, New Zealand's population is made up of people mostly from European origin, but also a large number of Maoris. There is a small minority of Pacific Islanders, Chinese and Indians. With all the different races living together, the country experiences some racial tensions, but much less compared to other areas of the world. New Zealand's society is very similar to Europe's, but it also contains some of the traditional Maori values and culture.

Daily Life

Education

New Zealand offers free public education which is mandatory from ages six through 16. At the age of five, children may attend pre-school which is state-funded but not required. Many private and religious primary and secondary schools are located throughout the country as well. Students who live in isolated areas receive an education through a correspondence school in Wellington.

The public primary schools are co-educational, but many of the secondary schools are segregated into all-boys or all-girls schools. After secondary school, most New Zealanders attend technical institutes, community colleges, or teachers' colleges. The country also offers several universities and an agricultural college.

Because the government places a strong emphasis on education, almost every New Zealander can read and write. The government provides many programs and resources for those who wish to continue lifelong education.

Urban vs. Rural New Zealand

Cities in New Zealand are generally not crowded and resemble most western cities with businesses, industries, fine art and educational facilities, entertainment, and architecture. Most city dwellers own their own homes, but some live in high-rise apartment buildings.

The rural population is made up of many farming communities. These farmers raise livestock (especially sheep), make dairy products, or grow fruit and vegetables. Vineyards in the south parts of the North Island grow the grapes that produce famous New Zealand wine.

Famous New Zealanders

Sir Edmund Hillary (1919 – 2008), an explorer and mountaineer, was one of the first two climbers to successfully reach the summit of Mount Everest in 1953. He and his climbing partner Tenzig Norgay were part of the ninth British expedition to Mount Everest.

Sir Peter Jackson (1961 –) is perhaps best known as writer, director, and producer of the *Lord of the Rings* movies. Born and raised near Wellington, Jackson has gone on to become one of the most successful members of the film-making industry.

Actor and musician Russell Crowe (1964 –) was born in New Zealand and grew up in Australia. He is an Academy Award-winning actor, and has starred in films such as *Gladiator*, *A Beautiful Mind*, *Cinderella Man*, and *Master and Commander*.

Mount Everest

Here are some fun facts about verbal and nonverbal communication in New Zealand.

Famous New Zealand Proverbs

Here are some famous New Zealand proverbs. What do you think they mean?

Survival is the treasured goal.

Let us keep close together, not far apart.

Don't lean on your fellow men – theirs is an ever moving support.

Who lives in a quiet house has plenty.

Boast during the day; be humble at night.

Though my present may be small, my love goes with it.

Many stars cannot be concealed by a small cloud.

In peace be faithful; in war be valiant.

Let someone else sing your praise.

Old canoes can be restored, but youth and beauty cannot.

The block of wood should not dictate to the carver.

Turn your face to the sun and the shadows fall behind you.

When one chief falls, another one rises.

A house full of people is a house full of different points of view.

A warrior dies in battle; a mountain climber on the rocks, but a farmer dies of old age.

A hand that is ready to hit may cause you great trouble.

The more you ask how much longer it will take, the longer the journey will seem.

Body Language and Etiquette in New Zealand

Here are some examples of body language and etiquette you'll find in New Zealand.

A traditional Maori greeting involves touching or lightly rubbing noses together. It is mostly used at formal events.

An arm's length of personal space is considered acceptable in most situations. People that are close, such as family or friends, may stand closer.

People in New Zealand are generally on time – punctuality is considered important in most social situations.

The raising of the eyebrows can be an informal way of greeting someone.

If invited to someone's home, it is polite to bring a small gift.

Know Before You Go

English is the most common language in New Zealand, but Maori can still be heard in parts of the country. Here are some common Maori phrases you might use in New Zealand. The spelling and pronunciation are also given. Try them out, and then look up some additional ones.

English	**Maori**	**Pronunciation**
Hello.	Kia ora.	kee OHR-rah
See you again.	Ka kite.	Kah KEE-teh
Good morning!	Morena!	MOH-rehn-ah
Good evening!	Pomarie!	poh-MAH-ree
Please	Koa	KOH-ah
Thank you!	Kia ora!	kee OHR-rah
one	tahi	tah-HEE
two	rua	ROO-uh
three	toru	TOH-roo
four	wha	fah
five	rima	REE-mah
six	ono	OH-no
seven	whitu	FIH-too
eight	waru	WAH-roo
nine	iwa	EE-wuh
ten	tekau	tek-OH

FOODS

New Zealand cuisine is based on a combination of traditional British dishes and the use of fresh local produce, meat and fish. Many New Zealand dishes feature venison, lamb, lobster, abalone, mussels, shellfish, sweet potatoes, and kiwifruit.

Traditional Maori cuisine also uses locally grown crops and farm-raised meats. One traditional meal, called the *hangi*, is cooked in a type of underground oven (*umu*). A deep hole is dug into the ground, and then lined with stones. The stones are then covered with leaves, sticks, and other vegetation. The ingredients are added next, and these can include meats (such as lamb, pork, or chicken) and vegetables (such as potatoes or sweet potatoes). Everything in the oven is sprinkled with water, covered with more vegetation, and allowed to steam for several hours. This great feast involves all members of the family, with each person taking on a different task in preparing the meal.

Restaurants, bistros, and cafés have been popping up all over New Zealand. A variety of international cuisines are available at restaurants, including Mediterranean, Asian, and Indian.

Here are a few common dishes in New Zealand cuisine:

pavlova – a sweet, meringue-based dessert with a crispy crust, often garnished with whipped cream and berries
lamingtons – chocolate or raspberry sponge cake that is filled with cream
boil up – pork, potatoes, and dumplings cooked together in a stew pot
fish and chips – deep-fried fish filet and fried potatoes
Anzac biscuits – sweet biscuits made using rolled oats, golden syrup, and coconut

Pavlova

Anzac Biscuits

Anzac Biscuits
1 cup rolled oats
1 cup white flour (sifted)
1 cup sugar
¾ cup shredded coconut
4 oz butter or margarine
2 tbsp light-colored pancake syrup, molasses, or treacle
½ tsp baking soda
1 tbsp boiling water

Combine oats, sifted flour, sugar, and coconut. Combine butter/margarine with syrup in sauce pan; stir over low heat until melted and thoroughly blended.

Mix baking soda with boiling water and add to butter and syrup mixture. Stir liquid mixture into dry ingredients until batter is formed.

Place teaspoons of batter onto a greased cookie sheet about 3 inches apart to allow for spreading. Bake in 350° oven for 20 minutes. Place biscuits on rack to cool.

Holidays & Festivals

As a primarily European culture, New Zealanders celebrate many of the same religious and secular holidays celebrated throughout the West. The following are celebrations that are unique to New Zealand.

Auckland Anniversary • *January*
This holiday celebrates the anniversary of New Zealand's largest city—Auckland. On this day, the annual Auckland Regatta takes place, an event that has been organized since 1840. In addition to the yachts racing on the water, there are plenty of land-based activities to ensure everyone has a great time!

Waitangi Day • *February 6*
Waitangi Day celebrates the signing of the Treaty of Waitangi, the document that made New Zealand part of the British Empire, in 1840. At dawn on Waitangi Day, the Royal New Zealand Navy raises the New Zealand Flag, Union Flag and St. George's Ensign. The ceremonies during the day include a church service and singing and dancing performances. Several Maori canoes and a navy ship also reenact the calling of Governor Hobson to sign the treaty. The day closes with a traditional ceremony of the flags being lowered by the Navy.

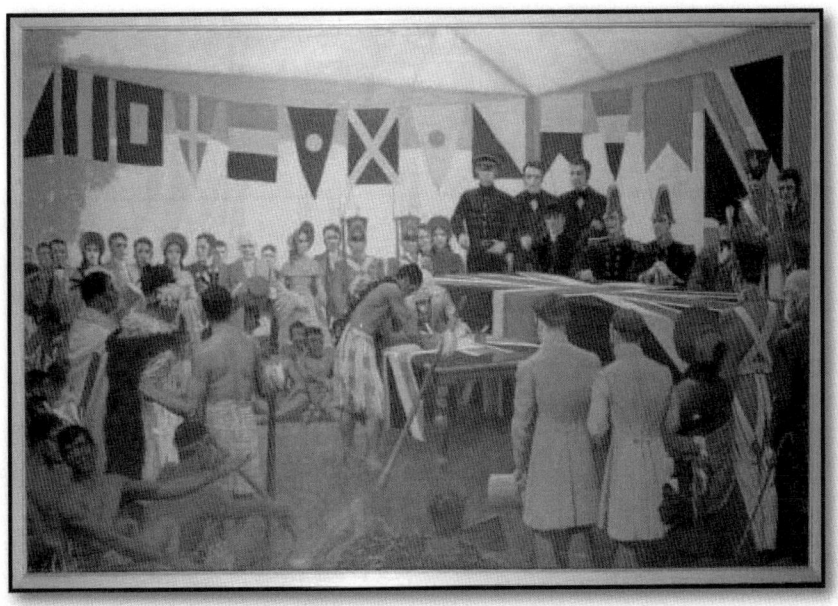

Signing of the Treaty of Waitangi

ANZAC Day • *April 25*
This national day of remembrance is celebrated in New Zealand and Australia to honor members of the Australian and New Zealand Army Corps (ANZAC) who fought at Gallipoli during World War I. Today the holiday commemorates everyone who served in military operations. Parades take place at dawn, and paper poppies are given out and worn as symbols of remembrance.

MP5124 - New Zealand

Creative Arts

Maori Art

In an effort to preserve Maori art and traditions, there has been a renaissance in Maori woodcarving, weaving, and architecture. Traditionally, Maori carvers would carve materials such as wood, bone, and shells, but today a wide variety of materials are used. Maori artists are venturing into more contemporary art styles, many with great success.

Literature

New Zealand has a famous literary history. The country is home to many famous writers of European descent. The most well-known of the historical writers was William Pember Reeves, and the most famous fictional writer was Katherine Mansfield. During the Great Depression, a group of poets set up a national tradition of writing. The most notable of these poets were Allen Curnow, A.R.D. Fairburn, and Charles Brasch. During this time, an author named Frank Sargeson began writing charming stories in New Zealand *vernacular*—a style of speech or slang unique to New Zealand. This earned him international recognition. Other writers have gained worldwide fame and have been expanding the country's literary culture ever since.

Frances Hodgkins

Painting

During the latter half of the 20th century, painting became especially popular in New Zealand. Painters such as Frances Hodgkins began to rival authors in artistic accomplishment. In the 1960s, an "Art Scene" emerged in New Zealand. Painters Colin McCahon and Don Biney produced beautiful modern works that showed the influence of international artists.

Performing Arts

New Zealand also has several successful professional theater companies and symphony orchestras. New Zealand's national orchestra (New Zealand Symphony Orchestra) tours the country and performs over 100 shows each year. The country has also produced several famous singers, including opera singer Kiri Te Kanawa.

Sports & Games

Rugby

Without a doubt, rugby is the most popular sport in New Zealand. The beloved national team, the All Blacks, won the first World Cup of rugby in 1987, when the country co-hosted the event. The opening of each All Black match features a performance of the *haka*, a traditional Maori chant accompanied by fierce movements and gestures, by the players.

Cricket

Cricket has been played in New Zealand since the 1830s. One of the most popular sports in the country, cricket is played both recreationally and professionally. In 2000, the women's national cricket team won the World Cup title against rival Australia.

Dave Gallaher, captain of the original All Black team

Outdoor Activities

Many New Zealanders enjoy sailing, surfing, fishing, and boating in the country's coastal waters and hunting in the inland forests. People also enjoy participating in adventure sports such as skiing and hiking, and New Zealand also helped popularize bungee jumping. The country's mountainous terrain attracts many hikers and climbers.

Papua New Guinea

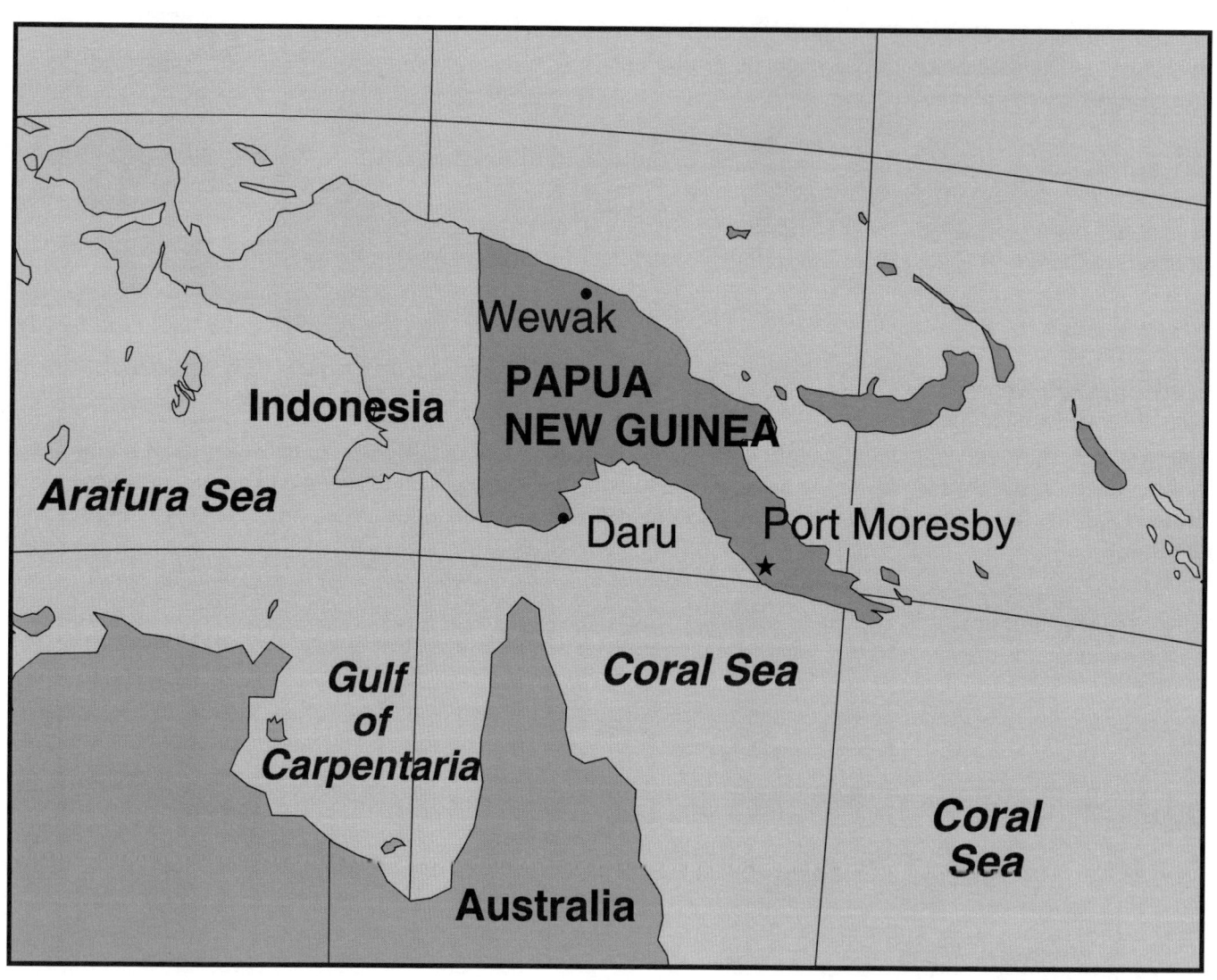

Welcome to Papua New Guinea!

Papua New Guinea is an independent nation located north of Australia in the Pacific Ocean. It is one of the least explored countries in the world. This nation includes the eastern half of the island of New Guinea along with a chain of tropical islands that covers over 1,000 miles of ocean.

FAST FACTS

Official Name: Independent State of Papua New Guinea

Location: Oceania; group of islands between the Coral Sea and the South Pacific Ocean

Population: 6,064,515 (2010 estimate)

Capital City: Port Moresby

Area: 178,704 square miles (462,840 square kilometers)

Major Language: Tok Pisin
English
Hiri Motu

Major Religion: Papua New Guinea is predominately Christian, but many people have combined their faith with indigenous beliefs and practices.

Currency: The *kina*   1 *kina* = 100 *toea*

Climate: Tropical; monsoon seasons; slight seasonal temperature variation

The Land: Mountains with coastal lowlands and rolling foothills

Type of Government: Constitutional monarchy

Flag: The flag of Papua New Guinea is divided diagonally into two triangular sections. The upper red section pictures a golden bird-of-paradise, and the lower black section has five stars representing the Southern Cross constellation.

Coat of Arms: In the center of the coat of arms is a bird-of-paradise. The bird is standing on a *kundu* drum, which is in front of a hunting spear.

National Animal: Raggiana Bird-of-Paradise

Motto: "Unity in diversity"

Natural Environment

Papua New Guinea is a tropical island with many mountains, forests, and swamps. The main wetland region is located near the Sepik and Fly rivers. The country's terrain is mostly mountainous, with foothills and lowlands near the coast. The highest peak (Mount Wilhem) reaches an elevation of 14,793 feet. The north coast of the island is home to many active volcanoes.

The country is located on the Pacific Ring of Fire—a place where different plates in the earth's crust rub together. This causes lots of earthquakes and tsunamis. Some of the islands in the Papua New Guinea chain are the tops of underwater mountains surrounded by beautiful coral reefs. Other main islands belonging to Papua New Guinea are New Ireland, New Britain, Manus, and Bougainville.

Papua New Guinea experiences a tropical climate—hot and humid temperatures that vary depending on elevation and region. The country has two monsoon seasons, one from December to March and the other from May to October. Papua New Guinea is one of the few regions near the equator that experiences snowfall. This does not happen often, and it only occurs in the inland mountains.

Like Australia and New Zealand, Papua New Guinea is home to many unique wildlife species. The country has several marsupials such as kangaroos and possums, and distinct birds like birds-of-paradise. It also has an abundance of unusual trees, such as the Araucaria pines, broadleafed southern beech, and other trees from families of Australian and Antarctic flora.

Papua New Guinea is rich in natural resources such as gas, oil, minerals, timber, fish, and agricultural products. Their most important exports are gold, copper, petroleum, coffee, and cocoa. Because Papua New Guinea is a tropical island, the government may try promoting it as a tourist attraction in the future, but as of now, there is not much of a tourism industry.

Raggiana Bird-of-Paradise

Because 80% of the country is covered in tropical rainforests, it is extremely difficult to construct roads. Some parts of Papua New Guinea can only be reached by air, on foot, or by canoe.

In Your Classroom

Make a copy of the Papua New Guinea flag to display in the classroom. Use poster board, pencils, crayons, markers, and paint. Hang the flag in a visible spot so students can refer to it while the class is studying the country.

Have the students find Papua New Guinea on a map. Give each student a copy of a map of the area and have them color the part of New Guinea and its outlying islands that belong to the nation of Papua New Guinea. Keep the maps handy so they can be accessed during the study of the country.

Look up all the countries' flags that have stars on them. Make a list or chart of what each country's stars symbolize.

A History of Papua New Guinea

People have lived in Papua New Guinea for thousands of years. The early inhabitants were some of the first in the world to develop agriculture. Some of their earliest crops were sugarcane, Pacific bananas, and yams. These early farmers used tools made from bone, wood, and stone. They set up trade with those located near the coast trading pottery and shell ornaments, and those from the interior trading forest products.

European Exploration

Spanish and Portuguese explorers arrived on the islands in the early 1500s. A navigator by the name of Don Jorge de Meneses is believed to have named the island *Papua*, which is a Malay word for *fuzzy hair*. The island became known as "New Guinea" a few decades later when a Spanish explorer named Íñigo Ortiz de Retes thought the people resembled those of Africa's Guinea coast. These Spanish and Portuguese sailors were soon followed by Dutch and English explorers who continued to visit Papua New Guinea over the next 300 years.

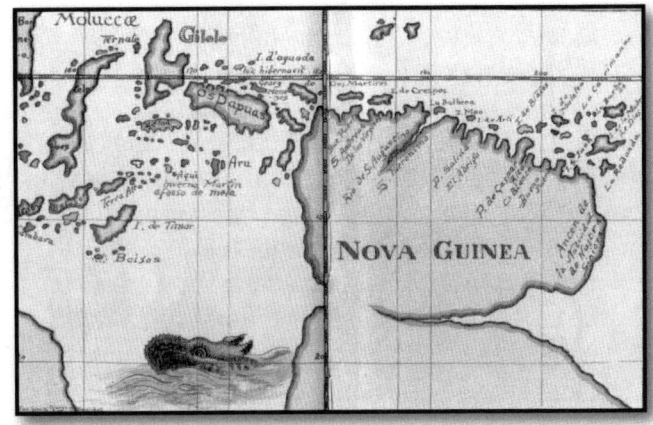

Germany annexed the northeastern part of New Guinea and its offshore islands in 1884. Later that year, Britain overtook southeastern New Guinea and its nearby islands. In 1906, Australia gained administrative control of Britain's part of the land and renamed it Territory of Papua. During World War I, Australia overtook the land that had formerly belonged to Germany. Following the war, the League of Nations officially put Australia in control of these islands. During World War II, however, Japanese soldiers invaded the islands and controlled much of the area. After the war, Australia united the region and placed it all under one government.

Independence

On September 16, 1975, the islands gained independence as the nation of Papua New Guinea. Their first prime minister, Michael Somare, held this and other positions of governmental leadership multiple times over the next 40 years. In 1988, conflicts about mining and land rights broke out on the island of Bougainville. These attacks soon grew into a huge rebellion, with the island fighting for its freedom. Around 20,000 people lost their lives because of the violence. After years of unrest, the rebel leaders and government leaders met and signed a cease-fire in 1998. In 2001, they signed a peace treaty granting Bougainville the right to rule itself. These leaders plan to meet again in the future to discuss whether the island should be granted its independence.

Today, most of the population is still located in rural parts of the country. Urbanization has increased somewhat over the last two decades, causing ethnic disputes, crime, unemployment, and other issues. The country continues to maintain close ties with Australia, and in recent years has begun cultivating ties with Asia.

Daily Life

Papua New Guinea is one of the world's least-explored countries. Most of the country's population lives in highland valleys that were not discovered by the outside world until the 1930s. These communities, or tribes, existed several thousands of years ago.

The People

Papua New Guineans place high importance on the bonds of kinship. They respect their immediate and distant family members and fulfill obligations like caring and providing for them. In villages, people earn their statuses and positions and are well respected.

Papua New Guinea is considered one of the most diverse countries in the world. Melanesians, Papuans, Negritos, Micronesians and Polynesians are only a few of the groups that live on the islands, in addition to the hundreds of indigenous groups. Many of the people live in the valleys of the country's interior highlands. The people belong to separate communities or tribes and speak their own unique language, and have their own distinct customs and traditions. These differences have caused minor conflicts between the tribes throughout history. A popular folk saying among Papua New Guineans is "for each village, a different culture."

Over 860 languages are spoken throughout Papua New Guinea. Most of these languages are unrelated to each other and have very complex grammar. To make communication easier, people learn *lingua francas,* or languages that are widely understood by everyone. In Papua New Guinea, the lingua francas are Pidgin English or Melanesian Pidgin, known as *Tok Pisin,* and Hiri Motu.

Although Papua New Guinea has a low population density, the crowded Chimbu Province in New Guinea's highlands averages 60 people per square mile. In some areas, as many as 200 people grow their crops on one square kilometer of land.

Agriculture

Farming has always been important to the people of Papua New Guinea. They were one of the first cultures to develop agriculture. Today, most people still live in the country and cultivate farms, living off their crops and products. It is no surprise, then, that the country's economy is based on agriculture. People live off the crops they grow, such as sweet potatoes, yams, and cassava. They also produce agricultural products to sell, such as cocoa, coconuts, coffee, palm oil, rubber, and tea.

Sweet potatoes

Most Papua New Guineans practice the traditional social structures of village life. These have been ingrained in them from an early age. One of the most important of these is the practice of subsistent economy. This means everyone grows enough food so their families will have enough to eat. The people have a very strong relationship with the land because it provides them with their livelihood. They share the land with each other and do not recognize ownership, even after land has been sold.

Education and Religion

Over the years, many missionaries have moved to Papua New Guinea to teach the natives about religion. Because of their influence, most of the population is Christian. These missionaries helped establish schools to educate the tribal children. About 60% of the population can read and write. Education is not mandatory. 80 percent of children attend primary school, but only 15% attend secondary school. The country offers six universities for those who wish to further their education.

About 2,000 American missionaries live in Papua New Guinea. The natives who are not Christian practice spirit worship and ancestor worship. They also believe in *masalai*, or evil spirits, which are blamed for doing bad things to people and causing sickness, death, and other problems.

Transportation

Because Papua New Guinea is so mountainous, travel is often very difficult. Air travel is the most important method of crossing long distances, and there are many airstrips around the country. Many of the smaller villages can only be reached on foot.

In Your Classroom

Discuss the meaning of *lingua franca*. Does the world have a *lingua franca*? If so, what language is that? Are there more than one?

Discuss the Papua New Guinean concept of communal or shared land. How would this work if we were to implement it in other parts of the world?

Body Language and Etiquette in Papua New Guinea

Here are some examples of body language and etiquette you'll find in Papua New Guinea.

> *Clasping hands and grabbing someone's waist are both common greetings. When meeting the head of a village, it is proper to bow.*
>
> *Crowding is not uncommon in public places. It is not considered rude to stand very close to others.*
>
> *"Melanesian time" refers to a more relaxed time schedule in Papua New Guinea. Being on time is not always necessary, and impromptu dinner invitations are not uncommon.*
>
> *People in Papua New Guinea will often point with their chins instead of hands or fingers.*
>
> *It is often considered rude to walk by a person and greet them without stopping for a chat. This suggests that you do not have time or care for the person.*

Know Before You Go

There are three official languages in Papua New Guinea: Tok Pisin, Hiri Motu, and English. Tok Pisin, often called Pidgin, is commonly heard around the country. Tok Pisin pronunciation is very similar to English.

Here are some common Tok Pisin phrases you will use in Papua New Guinea. The spelling and pronunciation are also given. Try them out, and then look up some additional ones!

English	Tok Pisin	Pronunciation
Hello.	Gude.	goo DAY
How are you?	Yu stap gut?	yoo stahp goot
Fine, thank you.	Mi stap gut.	mee stahp goot
What is your name?	Husat nem bilong yu?	HOO-zaht naym bee-LONG yoo?
My name is…	Nem bilong mi emi…	naym bee-LONG mee ehm-ee
Please	Plis	plees
Thank you!	Tenkyu!	TEHNK-yoo
You're welcome.	Nogat samting.	NOH-gaht sahm-ting
one	wan	wahn
two	tu	too
three	tri	tree
four	foa	FOH-ah
five	faiv	fighv
six	sikis	SIH-kiss
seven	seven	SEH-vehn
eight	et	ayt
nine	nain	nighn
ten	ten	tehn

FOODS

Agriculture is a very important part of daily life in Papua New Guinea, and is the source of most daily meals. Fruits such as bananas, mangoes, pineapples and coconuts, and vegetables like sweet potatoes, yams, *breadfruit*, and *taro* are considered staples. Starches such as rice and *wild sago* are frequently included in dishes.

A variety of meat is used in Papua New Guinean cooking, depending on the animals that are raised locally. Pork, fowl, and meat from marsupials and turtles are some of the meats that can be included in a meal. Coastal villages are able to catch and cook fish as well.

Most food is roasted or boiled, and villagers usually eat two meals a day. For special occasions, earthen ovens are dug into the ground and used to prepare the meal.

Here are a few common dishes in Papua New Guinean cuisine:

chicken pot – chicken with vegetables and coconut cream
dia – sago and bananas with coconut cream
kaukau – baked sweet potatoes
kol pis no rais – fish with rice
mumu – a traditional dish combining roasted pork, sweet potatoes, rice and greens

Sago palm tree

Tea is usually had with every meal, but coconut milk is another common drink.

Restaurants and fast food stands (called *kai bars*) are becoming more popular in Papua New Guinea. European, Indonesian, and Chinese restaurants can be seen in some of the country's larger towns and cities.

Holidays & Festivals

Each village practices its own distinct rituals. In the highlands, they have musical festivals known as *sing sing*. At these events, villagers paint their faces and bodies, wear feathers, pearls, and animal skins and reenact legendary battles.

Weddings are large celebrations in most villages. Brides are often bought with a dowry, or payment, which goes to her father. These dowries often include pigs, *cassowaries* (birds), or money. In some places, a bride must pay the dowry. Certain local customs require the groom to pay for the bride with a number of gold-edged clam shells. This tradition comes from the fact that Papua New Guineans used to use sea shells as currency until 1933.

Here are a few of the most popular Papua New Guinean festivals and celebrations:

National Mask Festival • *July*
This festival's goal is to promote the mask cultures of Papua New Guinea. During the festival, masks are showcased in a variety of different performances, and masks are put on display for visitors to view. The three major categories of masks shown are spirit masks, ancestor masks, and *tumbuan* masks (body masks that may cover the head, shoulders, and torso).

Hiri Moale Festival • *September 16*
This three-day cultural festival takes place every year in Port Moresby on Independence Day. The festival celebrates the hard ocean journeys made by the Motuan people, the original inhabitants of Port Moresby. Today the festival features an art show, dances, and a beauty pageant.

Goroka Show • *September*
Every year in the town of Goroka, nearly 100 indigenous tribes gather together to showcase their music, dance, and customs. The festival began in the 1950s, and has now become one of the few opportunities tourists have to see these types of traditional performances.

Creative Arts

Papua New Guinea has a rich tradition of carving, dancing, pottery, body decoration, hunting, and sea navigation. Because Papua New Guinea is made up of so many different cultural groups, there are countless unique styles of art, dance, weaponry, singing, music, architecture, and costumes. These styles are often put on display during *sing-sings* that take place around the country.

One of Papua New Guinea's richest traditions, wood carving, is usually made in the form of plants or animals that represent ancestors' spirits. The country is also famous for its hand-carved masks and canoes.

In Your Classroom

Search for 'Papua New Guinea Sing Sing" on the Internet. Show the students one of the many videos depicting a traditional sing-sing.

It is mentioned above that because of the large number of cultural groups in Papua New Guinea, 'there are countless unique styles of art, dance, weaponry, singing, music, architecture, and costumes.' Ask the students to create a Venn diagram showing the similarities and differences in creative arts between two different indigenous groups. Have them use the Internet, books, or other resources to find their information.

Have students design their own tribal masks. Ask each designer what his or her mask represents.

Sports & Games

Rugby is the most popular sport in Papua New Guinea. The local enthusiasm for the game is extremely intense. The locals treat it almost as though it is a matter of life and death. The country has an intense rivalry with Australia's national rugby team. Over 50% of Papua New Guinean men under the age of 20 play rugby.

Soccer, cricket, basketball, volleyball, and netball are also gaining popularity. Sports heroes, regardless of the sport they play, instantly become celebrities when they represent Papua New Guinea in professional leagues overseas.

Name _____ Date _____

Mapping Out Papua New Guinea

Follow the clues below to label the map of Papua New Guinea.

1. The capital of Papua New Guinea, **Port Moresby**, is located along the southern coast of the mainland.
2. One of four national parks, **McAdam National Park** is located just north of the Gulf of Papua.
3. **Bougainville Island** is the easternmost island of Papua New Guinea.
4. The highest mountain peak in the country, **Mount Wilhelm**, is directly north of McAdam National Park.
5. The annual Goroka Show takes place in the city of **Goroka**. This city can be found just to the east of Mount Wilhelm.
6. **New Britain** is a large island that has coasts on both the Solomon Sea and the Bismark Sea.
7. When traveling south from Wewak to Daru, you would probably pass through the town of **Mendi.**
8. **Verirati National Park** is located southeast of Port Moresby.

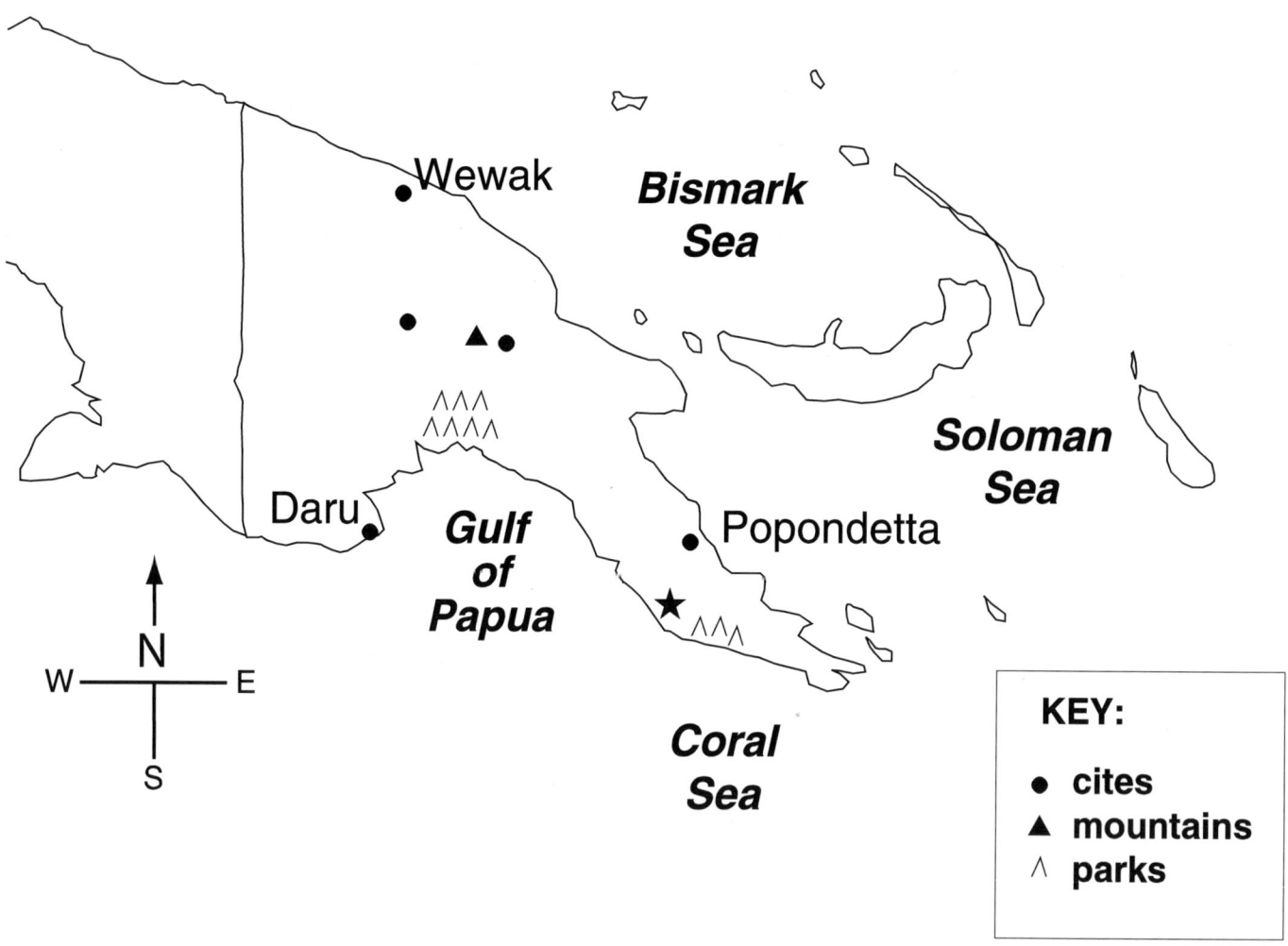

42

Papua New Guinea - MP5124

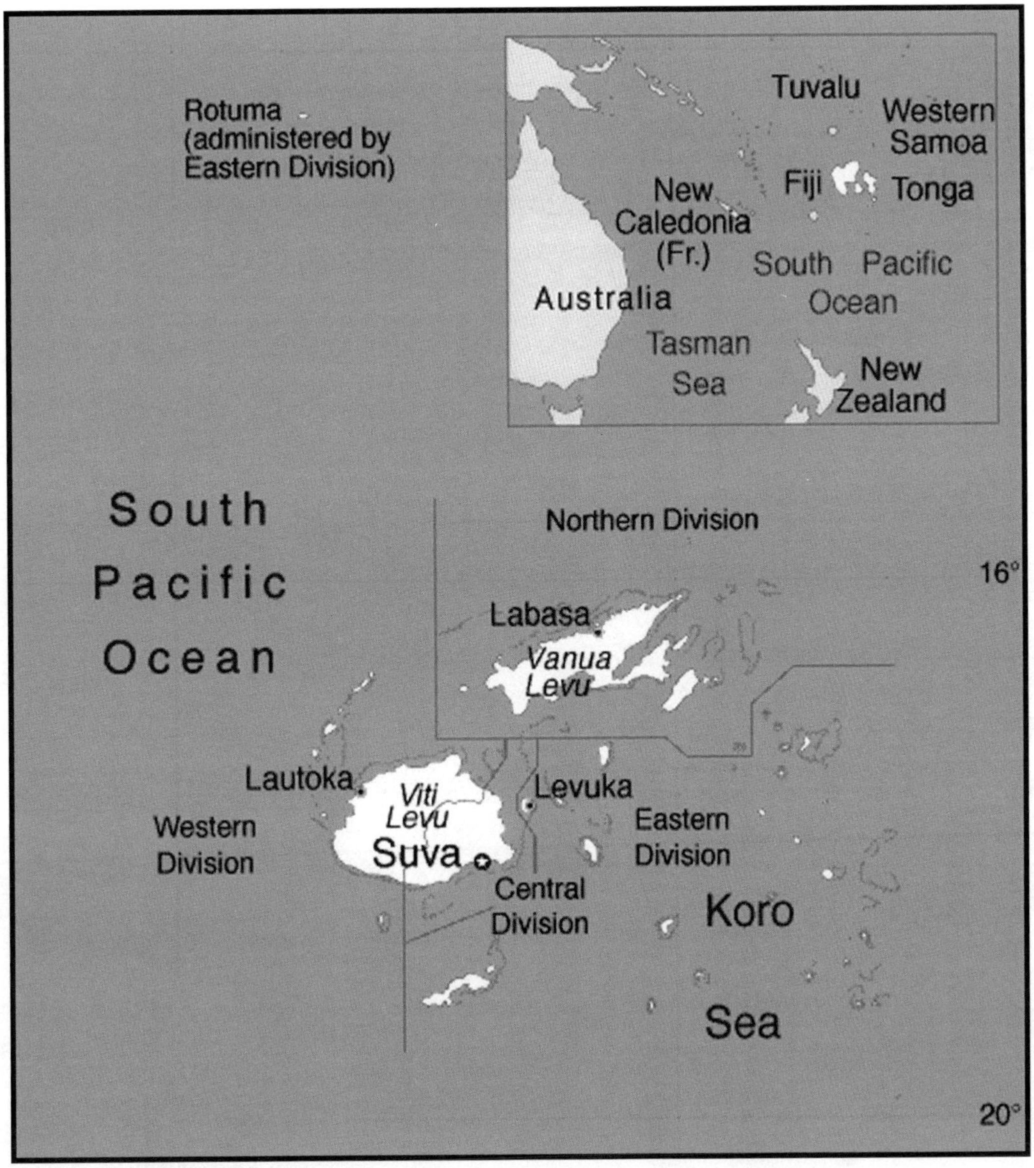
Rotuma
(administered by
Eastern Division)
Tuvalu
Western
Samoa
Fiji
Tonga
New
Caledonia
(Fr.)
South Pacific
Ocean
Australia
Tasman
Sea
New
Zealand
South
Pacific
Ocean
Northern Division
16°
Labasa
Vanua
Levu
Lautoka
Viti
Levu
Levuka
Western
Division
Suva
Eastern
Division
Central
Division
Koro
Sea
20°

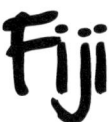

Welcome to Fiji!

Fiji is a beautiful country in the South Pacific. It is made up of more than 320 islands and hundreds of small islets and reefs. The country used to be a British colony, but is now an independent nation with a president and a prime minister. The Great Council of Chiefs, a traditional body of Fijian chiefs, appoints the president to serve for a five-year term. The president is the head of state and selects the prime minister, who is the head of the government. The prime minister chooses a cabinet to help him with his duties.

Fast Facts

Official Name: Republic of the Fiji Islands

Location: Oceania, in the South Pacific Ocean, about two-thirds of the way from Hawaii to New Zealand

Population: 875,983 (2010 estimate)

Capital City: Suva

Area: 7,056 square miles (18,274 square kilometers)

Major Languages: English and Fijian

Major Religion: Most ethnic Fijians are Christians, while most of the Indian population is Muslim or Hindi.

Currency: Fiji dollar   1 Fiji dollar = 100 cents

Climate: Tropical marine; slight seasonal temperature variation

The Land: Mostly mountains originating from volcanoes

Type of Government: Republic

Flag: The Fijian flag is light blue with the British Union Jack in its upper left corner. The right side of the flag pictures Fiji's coat of arms with a British lion, a dove, coconut palms, bananas, and sugarcane.

Coat of Arms: The shield contains images of Fiji's primary crops (sugarcane, a coconut palm, and bananas) as well as a dove of peace. The dove was an element of the flag of King Cakobau, the first King of Fiji. The English lion stands above the shield holding a cocoa pod in its paws. Two Fijian warriors stand next to the shield, one holding a lance and the other a pineapple mace. At the top of the crest is a wreath and a canoe. At the bottom of the crest is the country's motto.

National Flower: Tagimoucia

Motto: "Fear God and honor the King"

Natural Environment

The Republic of the Fiji Islands is made up of more than 320 islands, of which only about 100 are inhabited. Most of Fiji's islands were formed by volcanoes; others are made up of sand piled onto coral reefs. The largest island is Viti Levu, or "Big Fiji." This island covers half of Fiji's area. The second largest island, Vanua Levu, or "Big Land," covers a third of Fiji's area. Nearly all of the islands are surrounded by beautiful coral reefs. The larger islands' topography varies from rolling hills and low grasslands to high volcanic peaks. Over half of the country's land area is covered in tropical rainforests. The fertile coastal plains and river valleys are the best places for Fiji Islanders to raise their sugarcane, coconuts, and other crops.

Although Fiji is made up of tropical islands, the country's climate is quite comfortable. Cool winds refresh the air, keeping temperatures between 60 degrees and 90 degrees Fahrenheit. Fiji experiences a rainy season with many tropical storms between November and April.

Along with agricultural products, gold is an important export of Fiji. Timber, cement, building materials, cigarettes, and beer are other products manufactured in Fiji. Tourism is a major industry, as it provides many jobs for Fiji Islanders and brings many foreigners on vacation to the country to spend money.

Fiji's airport on Viti Levu experiences high volumes of air traffic with planes flying all over the Pacific. Because of this, its harbors, and its key position on major shipping routes, the country has been called "the crossroads of the South Pacific."

In Your Classroom

Locate a map of the Fiji Islands. Have the students copy their own map of Fiji and label the major cities and islands.

Using poster board, construction paper, scissors, glue, or paints, make a Fijian flag to hang in the classroom as you study the country.

Because Fiji is a popular tourist destination, it is easy to find many pictures of the country. Bring magazines with pictures from Fiji and have the students cut these out and hang them on the wall, making a classroom mural.

Create a Power Point presentation with pictures of Fiji. Show this to the class and discuss the students' observations.

Name _____ Date _____

Welcome to Fiji!

Fiji is a very popular tourist destination. Thousands of visitors travel to the island every year to enjoy the beautiful beaches and tropical weather.

Create an informative travel brochure about Fiji to share with your classmates.

Materials Needed:
- blank sheet of 8 1/2 x 11" paper
- markers or colored pencils
- research materials (books, articles, Internet access, etc.)

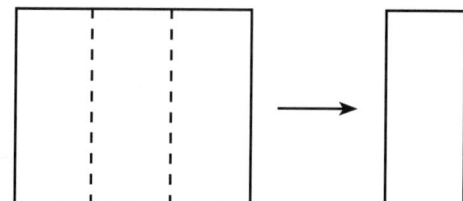

Begin by folding your paper in thirds, as shown.

Use books, magazines, Internet articles and other resources to find out more about islands of Fiji.

Illustrate the front cover of the brochure. Include the following information about Fiji on the inside pages of your brochure:

1. Where is Fiji located?

   _____

2. Name three important facts about Fiji.

   _____

   _____

   _____

3. What activities are there to do in Fiji?

   _____

   _____

   _____

4. Why should people visit Fiji?

   _____

   _____

   _____

Include pictures and any other information. Share your brochure with your classmates to learn even more about Fiji.

A History of Fiji

Early History

Fiji's early history is complicated and filled with many unknowns. The earliest inhabitants of Fiji were thought to have arrived from Vanuatu around 1220 BCE, but they did not stay on the island for long. Later, Melanesian, Polynesian and Micronesian people migrated to Fiji and assimilated with the people already living on the islands. An increase in population around 500 BCE led to more fighting amongst the tribes forming on the islands. Cannibalism and constant violent warfare were not uncommon at this time.

European Exploration

For centuries, the island nation remained relatively isolated. Explorers feared not only the brutal lifestyle of the islands' inhabitants, but the area was also surrounded by large, dangerous coral reefs. In 1643, Dutch explorer Abel Tasman became the first European to sail past the Fiji Islands. His descriptions of the treacherous reefs deterred other explorers for nearly 130 years. In 1774, famous British explorer Captain James Cook visited one of Fiji's southern islands, and in 1789, Captain Bligh (a castaway from the famous mutiny on the *Bounty*) passed between Viti Levu and Vanua Levu.

Over the next century, other outsiders began to arrive in Fiji. British merchants set up trading posts on the islands and traded sandalwood, sea cucumbers, *kula* feathers, *masi* (printed bark cloth), and weapons. Missionaries settled in the country. Also, many Australian convicts escaped to Fiji.

Blackbirding and Indentured Workers

The American Civil War (1861–1865) created a worldwide cotton shortage. Fiji responded by increasing the amount of cotton grown. This also resulted in a process called *blackbirding* – tricking or kidnapping people to work as laborers on farms and plantations. People often agreed to work for a certain amount of time in exchange for false promises of food, clothing, and return passage. Tribal chiefs were often bribed, and workers were even traded for ammunition. Later, blackbirding became a type of organized kidnapping.

Chief Cakobau

Fighting between numerous Fijian tribes continued. In 1871, Chief Cakobau (known to foreigners as King of Fiji) united the natives. With the help of King George Tupou I from the neighboring country of Tonga, Cakobau brought peace to the land. Cakobau worked out an agreement with Britain to make Fiji one of its colonies. This way, Fiji land rights would be protected against purchase by other countries. Fiji became a crown colony on October 10, 1874.

Crops such as cotton and sugar cane had become very important to Fiji's economy. To satisfy the need for an inexpensive workforce, indentured laborers were contracted from India. About 2,000 people arrived in Fiji each year for this purpose, and many chose to stay longer than their five contracted years. By 1919, when the indenture system ended, more than 60,000 indentured laborers had come to Fiji.

Independence

After being a British crown colony for 96 years, Fiji became an independent nation on October 10, 1970. The government helped the economy expand by developing manufacturing and forestry industries. It also increased the number of agricultural products so that other crops (besides sugar cane and cotton) could be grown. The government also began making Fiji a popular tourist destination. But unfortunately, racial tension between native Fijians and Indians was also growing.

Typically, native Fijians had held the most power in the government, including a win in the first post-independence election. In 1987, however, an Indian-dominated coalition won the majority. The new Prime Minister, a Fijian named Timoci Bavadra, selected a mixed-race cabinet. This caused controversy throughout the country. Bavadra was overthrown by angry ethnic Fijians who wanted to maintain control in the government. In 1990, Fiji adopted a Constitution that gave the power only to ethnic Fijians. This law lasted for several years, but was amended in 1997. The amendment gave political power to everyone. Two years later, the country elected its first Indian prime minister, Mahendra Chaudhry.

Modern Times

In 2000, Chaudhry and his cabinet were held hostage by rebels who resented the fact that native Fijians no longer controlled the government. The Fijian military took over the government and abolished the amendment from 1997, restoring control to ethnic Fijians. Several weeks later, Chaudhry and the other hostages from his cabinet were freed and the amendment was reinstated. A new, temporary government was established until the next elections. When these took place in 2001, a Fijian-backed party won the majority and regained their power. This ruling body was overthrown by yet another military coup in 2006. The leader of the coup, Commodore Voreqe Bainimarama, took control of the government.

The government of Fiji continues to be unstable, filled with new leaders and officials, political parties, voting systems, and legislation. Hopefully leaders will work together in the coming years to restore this island nation to a state of order and peace.

Daily Life

People of Fiji

Nearly half of Fiji's population is native Fijian. Most of these are Melanesian descendents. The rest of the population is of Indian origin, descendents of laborers who were brought into the country to work on plantations between 1879 and 1916. A small percentage of people from Chinese, European, Polynesian, and Micronesian backgrounds also live in Fiji.

Architecture of Fiji

Most Fiji Islanders, especially those living in cities and towns, live in modern homes that can be seen in any island country. Many of the islands contain beautiful resorts and hotels. Smaller towns usually have a single main street with shops on both sides. Many of these towns still maintain much of their British-style colonial architecture.

About 60% of ethnic Fijians live in rural areas. The traditional Fijian village contains several specific buildings: the *bure kalou*, or the temple, which is the tallest building in the village; the *lali* hut, a small shelter that protects a ceremonial gong; the *vale levu*, or chief's house, which is the largest structure in the village; the *vale ni bose*, or meeting house; the *vale ni qase*, where grandparents of the village stay during the day with the grandchildren; and the *vale ni kuro*, or the kitchen area. Families typically live in huts made of reed walls and a thatched roof called *na bure*.

Fijian temple

Going to School

English is the official language of Fiji and is used to teach students in school. Two other languages, Fijian and Hindi, are also used throughout the country. School is not mandatory, but over 85% of children from ages six to 13 attend school. These schools are typically segregated, with Indian children attending separate schools from Fijian children.

Schooling is divided into primary, secondary, and higher education. Students attend primary school for eight years, followed by five years in secondary school. Entrance into secondary school requires passing a competitive exam.

Fiji only has one university—the University of the South Pacific. This university is located in Fiji's capital city of Suva and is filled with students from all over the South Pacific islands.

The academic year in Fiji normally begins in February and ends with exams in November. The second semester usually begins in late July.

Transportation

Buses are the most common (and the least expensive) mode of transportation in Fiji. They travel between cities and towns on most of the inhabited islands. Bus stations are often the central hub of a small town. Some locals drive small cars or trucks.

To travel between islands, people most often choose to travel by ferry. Fiji also has several internal airlines that fly passengers from one island to another.

Famous Fijians

Ratu Sir Lala Sukuna (1888–1958), a native Fijian, was one of the most important figures in Fiji's road to independence. A college graduate (something that was unheard of at this time in Fiji), a war hero and a statesman, Sukuna worked with the people of Fiji to help them understand the changes needed to become a stable, independent nation. He held many positions in the Fijian government, and after his death, a national holiday was proclaimed in his name.

Professional golfer Vijay Singh (1963–) was born in Lautoka, Fiji. Nicknamed "The Big Fijian," Vijay has won three major golf championships, including the Masters in 2000 and the PGA Championship in 1998 and 2004. He was inducted into the World Golf Hall of Fame in 2006.

In Your Classroom

Discuss the racial problems in Fiji. Talk about the similarities between their racial tension and any racial tension that exists in your country. Emphasize the problem with one race forcing another to be their laborers.

Have your students draw a map of a typical Fijian village. Then have them compare and contrast, using a Venn diagram, the parts of the village to the city or town in which they live. Use books and other resources to help find additional information.

Ratu Sir Lala Sukuna's story is very unique and filled with adventures. Ask the students to use the Internet and other resources to help them write a brief biography of Ratu Sukuna. Ask the students to choose what they think is the most important achievement made by this great man.

Language & Expressions

Here are some fun facts about verbal and nonverbal communication in Fiji.

Famous Fijian Proverbs

Here are three famous Fijian proverbs. What do you think they mean?

Each bay, its own wind.
Idleness is to be dead at the limbs but alive within.
Life is like this: sometimes sun, sometimes rain.

Body Language and Etiquette in Fiji

Here are some examples of body language and etiquette you'll find in Fiji.

Speak softly – loud voices will be interpreted as expressing anger.

When visiting a village, it is customary to present a gift of kava.

When meeting new people, it is proper to shake hands and answer any questions asked. These questions may include, "Where are you from?" and "How many children do you have?"

People physically stand closer together in conversation than people do in North America, and they may even touch each other while talking.

Hats are not worn in villages. It is considered an insult to the chief.

Shoes are not worn inside the house.

It is considered an insult to touch someone's head.

When visiting a village, it is important to dress modestly. Showing too much skin is considered offensive.

If a person gives many compliments to a Fijian about an item he or she owns, the Fijian may feel obliged to give that person the item, whether they can afford to or not.

In rural areas, people do not pass by each other without expressing a greeting.

Gift giving is a complex system in Fiji. Whale teeth (also called tabua) are the most precious gift to be given. Tabua can be given at marriages, funerals, and other important occasions.

Know Before You Go

Nearly everyone in Fiji speaks English, as it is the official language. The Fijian language is still spoken in many parts of the country, and many Fijian terms are used in everyday English conversations.

Fijian pronunciation is very similar to English. Here are a few small changes:

a	is	ah	as in	water
b	is	mb	as in	amber
c	is	th	as in	the
d	is	nd	as in	windy
g	is	ng	as in	hunger

Here are some common phrases you will use in Fiji. The spelling and pronunciation are also given. Try them out, and then look up some additional ones.

English	**Fijian**	**Pronunciation**
Good morning.	Ni sa yadra.	nee sah yahn drah
Hello.	Bula.	mbula
Goodbye.	Ni sa moce.	nee sah moh they
Please	Yalo vinaka	yah loh vee nah kah
Thank you!	Vinaka!	vee nah kah
Excuse me.	Tulou.	too loh
Yes	Io	ee oh
No	seqa	sehn gah
one	dua	doo ah
two	rua	roo ah
three	tolu	toh loo
four	va	vah
five	lima	lee mah
six	ono	oh noh
seven	vitu	vee too
eight	walu	wah loo
nine	ciwa	thee wah
ten	tini	tee nee

MP5124 - Fiji

Foods

Passion fruit

Food in Fiji is a wonderful mix of the coconuts, fish, and various vegetables of the islands and the curries, rice, and bread of the Indian population. People in Fiji tend to eat three meals a day, but, as with most people, snacking is not uncommon! Meals are meant to be shared, and the evening meal generally requires the presence of all family members before beginning. In rural parts of the country, meals are served on a table cloth that is spread over a floor mat in the house.

Many Fiji Islanders, especially those in villages, grow their own fruits and vegetables. Fruits such as bananas, oranges, breadfruit, papayas, and passion fruit are common. Eggplant, sweet potatoes, beans, yams, and taro are some of the vegetables grown and used in meals. In addition to fruits and vegetables, many families also grow their own herbs, including curry leaves, coriander, and basil.

Meat (such as beef or pork), poultry, and fish can also be used in cooking when they are available, and is often served as the main course of the meal. Fish is often marinated in coconut cream as part of its preparation. Many Indo-Fijian dishes do not include certain meats due to religious dietary restrictions.

Lovo is a Fijian meal that is prepared for special occasions such as festivals and weddings. A type of underground oven is created by digging a hole in the earth and lining the hole with coconut husks. The husks are then lit on fire and covered by stones. Meats, fish and vegetables are wrapped in banana leaves and then placed on the heated stones. The packets are then cooked for over two hours.

Here are a few other traditional Fijian dishes:

duruka – an asparagus-like vegetable dish that is made with coconut cream

kassaua – a dish made from boiled or baked tapioca and cooked with coconut cream and mashed bananas. This dish is most often served at festivals.

kokodo – raw *mahi mahi* (fish) marinated in coconut cream, lime, tomatoes, and onions

With meals, water is the most common beverage. Fruit juices and coconut water may also be served, and tea is another drink option. The national drink of Fiji is *kava*, which is prepared by pounding the roots of the kava plant in a wooden bowl.

Restaurants, food stalls, tea shops and kava bars are found in towns across the country. In larger towns, restaurants featuring a wide variety of international cuisine are common. In addition to Fijian and Indo-Fijian restaurants, Chinese, Japanese, Korean, French, and American fast food restaurants serve locals and tourists alike.

Holidays & Festivals

New Year's Day • *January 1*
New Year celebrations in Fiji are similar to those in other parts of the world. The major difference is that New Year's Day festivities have been known to last a week or up to a month in various cities around the country.

National Youth Day • *Last Monday of March*
National Youth Day commemorates the importance of children in the building of Fiji as a nation. On this day, activities are planned by youth groups and various organizations across the country. Dance groups are formed to entertain the public, and short concerts are also performed. During the festivities, the government recognizes youth that have made valuable social contributions to the country.

Ratu Sukuna Day • *Last Monday of May*
This holiday celebrates Ratu Sir Lala Sukuna, who was widely considered to be a leader in readying Fiji for post-British independence. Celebrations on this holiday promote unity as well as diversity in Fiji. Community and national leaders give speeches, and people may choose to visit museum exhibits created in Ratu Sukuna's honor.

Fiji Day • *October 10*
This holiday celebrates the signing of the 1874 Deed of Cessation, which eventually led to the independence of the island nation in 1970. The main events take place in the cities of Levuka (on the island Ovalau) and the capital city, Suva. On this day, Fijians dress up in traditional costumes and reenact the signing of the deed. In Suva, people gather to hear speeches delivered by the president and prime minister. This is followed by a military parade and a ceremonial firing of cannons. Throughout the country, people hold contests and stage performances celebrating the day.

Diwali • *Typically October or November*
This five-day Hindu celebration takes place all over the world. Also called the Festival of Lights, Diwali is primarily celebrated by Indo-Fijians, but all Fiji Islanders are welcome to participate in the festivities. Its origins are based in Hindu mythology, and involve the return of a king to his kingdom after 14 years of exile. During the festival, people exchange small gifts and sweets to show their love and affection for each other. Extensive lighting and candle decorations are hung. Diwali is also celebrated in many schools in Fiji so that children may learn more about their own multicultural society.

Festivals

Sugar Festival (Date Varies)
Lautoka is a town known for its sugar production, and the Sugar Festival honors this important industry in Fiji. Every year, locals and visitors gather to watch the colorful parades, and children spend their time riding carnival-type rides. A pageant is held to find that year's newest Sugar Queen.

Diwali lantern

Bula Festival (Date Varies)
The Bula Festival (*bula* means *hello* in Fijian) is held in the town of Nadi. Parades featuring local marching bands, beauty pageants, and dancing contests are held to entertain the crowds. Horseracing is very popular on Nadi, and races occur frequently during the festival. One of the main goals of the Bula Festival is to help raise money for charity.

Hibiscus Festival (First week of August)
The Hibiscus Festival takes place every year in the town of Suva. Like the Bula Festival, the Hibiscus Festival features parades and beauty pageants. The highlight of the festival is the extravagant Hibiscus Ball.

The government of Fiji has created three organizations to help support the various cultural arts: the Fiji Museum, the National Trust of Fiji, and the Fiji Arts Council. The Fiji Museum displays and preserves the culture and history of the people of Fiji. The National Trust of Fiji is responsible for protecting the important historical sites of Fiji as well as the endangered species of plants and animals found on the islands. Finally, the Fiji Arts Council promotes the works of craftspeople and artists, including visual, performance, and fine arts.

Arts and Crafts

Many different types of crafts are handmade in Fiji – some for use in daily life, some to be used during ceremonies and other special events, and others to be sold to tourists. Men and women typically specialize in different crafts.

Female Crafts
Most Fijian women learn how to weave, and baskets, mats, and rope are created this way. Different regions of Fiji specialize in different styles of pottery, much of which is very elaborate. *Tapa* is a cloth made from the bark of the mulberry tree. Tapa is decorated with charcoal in special designs, and then given as gifts on special occasions.

Male Crafts
The carving of weapons such as clubs, spears, and hooks was very important in times of war, but men now primarily carve these items to be sold to tourists. Another craft, which was far more common several decades ago, is canoe building. Fijian men would build canoes not only for transportation, but also to be used in battle and during special ceremonies.

Meke

Meke is the traditional dance theater of Fiji. It combines singing, chanting, drumming, and dancing to tell stories of important events in history. Traditionally, a meke was said to have been an oracle of the gods, and the writer was thought to have gone into a trance while writing it. A meke may have been performed in villages in honor of a visit by a chief or during a ceremonial gift exchange. A modern meke might be written and performed to celebrate a special event.

Clothing

Traditional Fijian clothing consisted of loincloths and grass skirts of various lengths. Today, both men and women of Fiji wear a *sulu*, which is similar to a skirt. Men often pair the sulu (which hangs just below the knees) with a shirt and tie. Women wear a long sulu beneath a shorter dress. Fijian women tend to wear very brightly colored, and often patterned, clothing.

Many Indian women in Fiji wear *saris*, or brightly colored fabric wrapped around their bodies to form a long dress. Gold jewelry is often worn as an accessory to these beautiful garments.

The younger generation on the islands will often wear more Westernized clothing, including jeans, shorts, and t-shirts.

Sports & Games

Rugby

Rugby is Fiji's national sport and by far the most popular. The Fiji Rugby Union is made up of 36 clubs based all over the country. The national rugby team of Fiji, called Fiji Bati, competes in both the Rugby League World Cup and the Pacific Cup. In addition, primary and secondary schools in Fiji also have rugby teams on which students can play.

Football

Football (soccer) is a close second favorite, especially with the Indian community within the Fijian population. Like rugby, there are both professional and recreational football leagues in Fiji. Originally brought to Fiji by missionaries in the 1800s, football has grown from a leisurely game played by farmers and mill workers to a sport played by a national team that competes in tournaments such as the World Cup.

Other Sports

Outrigger paddling, a type of canoe race, has recently become a competitive sport that often has many participants. Cricket, surfing, boxing, and martial arts are also popular. Fiji's Vijay Singh is one of the top golfers in the world and has helped to popularize the sport among the islands.

Because Fiji is such a popular tourist destination, water sports are also very popular. People travel from all over the world to experience snorkeling and scuba diving in Fiji's numerous coral reefs. Surfing, sailing, canoeing, kayaking, and water skiing are also enjoyed at various resorts and hotels along the coast.

MP5124 - Fiji

Antarctica

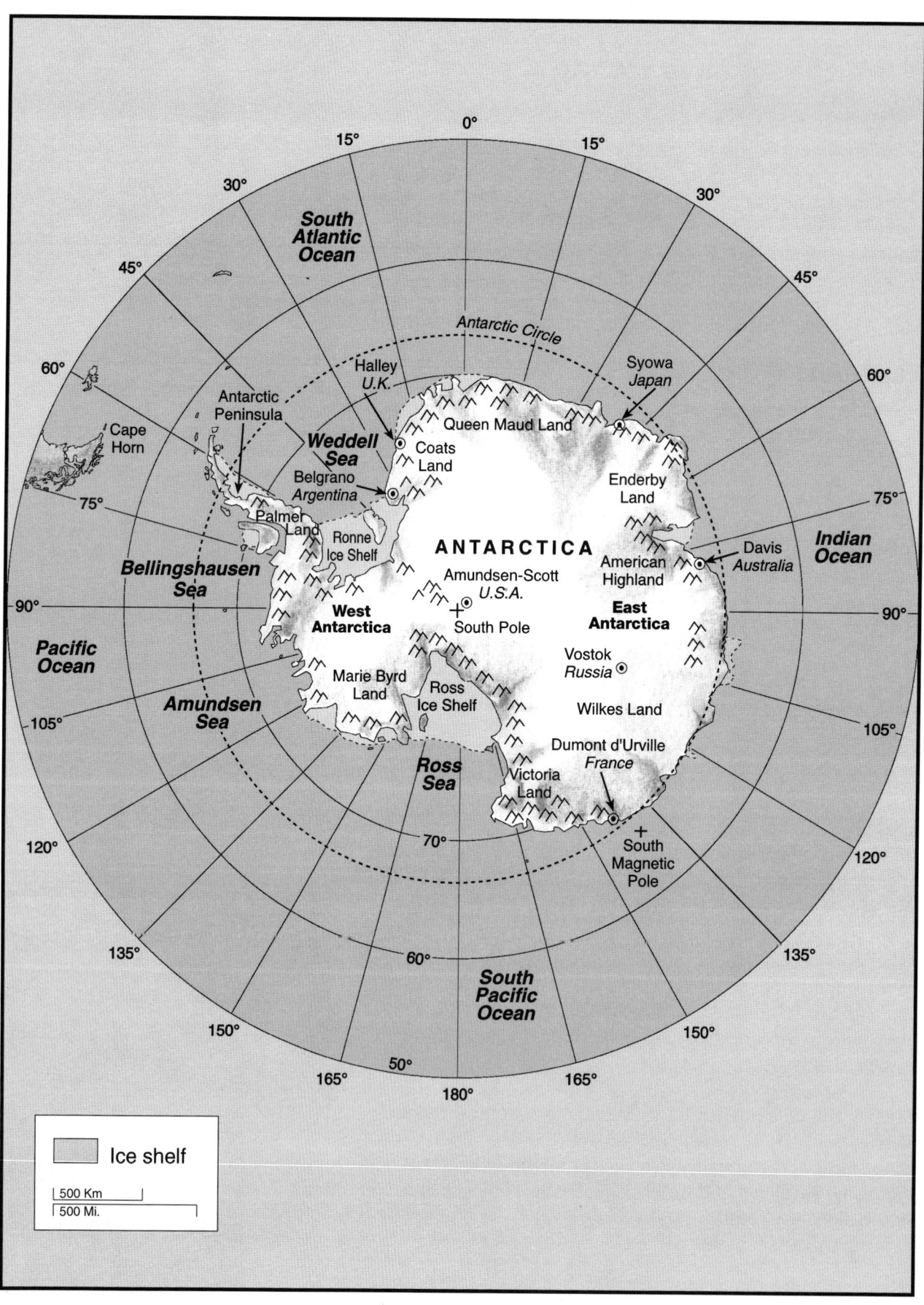

Welcome to Antarctica!

Antarctica is a large, cold continent buried in ice. The land is larger than Europe or Australia and is mostly dry and barren. The South Pole is located in its center, which is even colder than the North Pole. Antarctica is covered by two sheets of ice which are separated by the Transantarctic Mountains. The thickness of these layers of ice averages about 7,100 feet.

Antarctica is the highest continent in the world, averaging an elevation of 7,500 feet above sea level. Because of its extreme conditions, it is isolated from other continents. Planes that fly there must land on runways of solid ice, and ships that venture there must steer around massive icebergs along the coast. Temperatures never rise above freezing. In fact, the coldest temperature in the world (-128.6 degrees Fahrenheit) was recorded there.

Official Name: Antarctica

Location: Continent mostly south of the Antarctic Circle

Population: This varies because the only people living on the continent are scientific researchers.

Area: 5,400,000 sq. mi. (14,000,000 sq. km.), slightly less than 1.5 times the size of the United States

Climate: Severe low temperatures that vary with latitude, elevation, and distance from the ocean

The Land: About 98% thick ice sheet and 2% barren rock

Type of Government: The Antarctic region is governed by a system known as the Antarctic Treaty System.

Natural Environment

Geologists believe Antarctica used to be a part of a giant supercontinent known as Gondwanaland. This continent was made up of Antarctica, Africa, Australia, India, and South America. Many, many years ago, they believe this large continent began to break apart and the pieces of the continent slowly drifted to their present locations.

The Southern Ocean that surrounds Antarctica joins with the warmer, saltier northern waters to create a band of water called the Antarctic Convergence. A current known as the Antarctic Circumpolar Current flows from east to west around the continent.

Ninety-eight percent of Antarctica is covered in snow; the only visible parts of the land are tall mountain peaks and several bare, rocky areas. But underneath the layers of ice, Antarctica is similar to other continents. It has chains of mountains, valleys, and riverbeds.

Antarctica did not always used to be covered in ice. Scientists have discovered fossils of trees, dinosaurs, and other wildlife that used to live there. Eventually, glaciers began to form around the South Pole. They grew rapidly and soon covered the whole continent in thick layers of ice and snow, making Antarctica the frozen continent it is today.

Two thick layers of snow and ice cover most of Antarctica. These are known as the Antarctic sheets and were formed by layers of snow that were pressed together over many centuries. As the layers of snow hardened into ice, air that was trapped between pieces of snow formed bubbles. Today these air pockets give scientists important clues about past climates.

The Antarctic Sheets make up the largest body of ice (or fresh water) in the world. Their volume is over 7.25 million cubic miles, which makes up 70% of the world's fresh water. The thickest parts of the sheets are 11,500 feet, and the highest point reaches an elevation of 13,500 feet above sea level. If Antarctica's ice melted, oceans around the word would rise almost 230 feet, causing devastating floods to coastal cities. Because of the heavy weight of the inland ice sheets, ice at the coast moves about 660 feet per year. The glaciers move more quickly than the ice sheets, and some have deep cracks that can pose dangerous hazards to visitors.

Transantarctic Mountains

A mountain chain known as the Transantarctic Mountains spans the length of the continent. Some of these mountains are over 14,000 feet tall. Dry valleys once carved by glaciers can be found in between some of the steep peaks. Because of strong winds, any snow that falls in these valleys is blown away. A few of the valleys have lakes, but most are barren.

Lake Fryxell

The Transantarctic Mountains separate the two sheets of ice, dividing Antarctica into two regions. East Antarctica covers over half of the continent. Mountains, valleys, and glaciers line its coast while its interior contains an ice plateau 10,000 feet above sea level. This plateau is a polar desert and contains Antarctica's thickest ice. Strong winds blow the snow into ridges, or *sastrugi*, up to six feet in height along the plateau. The South Pole, the southernmost part of the earth, is located in the center of this plateau. East Antarctica is also home to the magnetic pole, which is the farthest point on earth in which a magnet will pull or a compass will point south. Every year, this pole moves slightly.

West Antarctica's ice sheet fills deep caverns and valleys. If this ice melted, West Antarctica would become a chain of islands. The mountainous S-shaped Antarctic Peninsula juts out from the western part of this continent. The mountains on this peninsula are a continuation of the Andes Mountains of South America. Many islands that early explorers believed to be Antarctica are located just offshore from the Antarctic Peninsula. The South Shetland Islands are located here and include Deception Island, which is home to an active volcano.

Other volcanoes and mountain ranges can be found in West Antarctica. Antarctica's highest peak, Vinson Massif, is located here and reaches an elevation of 16,864 feet. Mount Erebus, the continent's most active volcano, is located on an island just off the coast of West Antarctica. This island faces New Zealand and is known as Ross Island. The volcano is 12,448 feet high and sometimes spurts out pieces of volcanic rock along with lava.

Mount Erebus

Climate

Antarctica's climate is cold and dry. Its plateau is a polar desert, experiencing icy winds averaging 44 miles per hour. The coastal areas are less dry with slightly milder climates, and can experience winds up to 120 miles per hour. The interior part of the continent receives only about two inches of snowfall per year while the coastal regions receive about 24 inches per year. Islands in the north have summer temperatures reaching up to 50 degrees Fahrenheit. The summer months are November through February, and the winter months last from May through September. During several of these months, Antarctica is in constant darkness because of its extreme southern location.

Due to the harsh climate, few plants grow on the continent. The most common plants are mosses which cling to rocky areas along the coast. Another type of plant is a grass that grows on sunny slopes, forming dense mats. A flowering herb grows in small cushion-like bunches around the continent. Occasionally, one can spot pink or green algae growing on snow, lakes, or ice.

Animal and Plant Life

Not many animals can survive on Antarctica's mainland. A few insects and small animals can be found there, and most of them live at the edge of the continent. The largest of these land animals is a type of fly called a *wingless midge*, which is about ½ inch long. Lice, mites, and ticks cling to birds' feathers, seals' fur, and mosses in order to keep warm enough to survive.

Although few animals live on the continent, many live in the oceans surrounding it. Small shrimp-like creatures known as krill swim in the coastal waters, feeding on floating organisms. Other larger animals depend on krill for food, and in some countries people eat it as well.

A hundred types of fish abound in the Antarctic waters, including ice fish, plunderfish and Antarctic cod. During the summer, several kinds of whales migrate to these waters to feed on krill. These include fin whales, humpbacks, mikes, right whales, and the largest mammals on earth—blue whales, which can grow to a length of 100 feet. Killer whales live around Antarctica, too, feeding on the seals, penguins and smaller whales that can be found there.

Seals are other animals that live in Antarctic waters. They nest on the coast or on nearby islands, but spend most of their time in the water swimming, diving, and catching food. The southern elephant seal is the largest seal in the world and lives in Antarctica, feeding on squid. Male southern elephant seals can be up to sixteen feet long. Other seals such as the Weddell, Ross, crabeater, leopard, and Antarctic fur seal also live in this region. Leopard seals eat penguins as well as other seals.

Probably the most well-known Antarctic animal is the penguin. Because they cannot fly, penguins waddle awkwardly when they walk on land. In the water, however, they are skillful swimmers. Penguins can dive and swim very fast in search of fish and other food. Antarctica is home to six different breeds: the Adèlie (which is the most common), emperor penguins, chinstrap, gentoo, king, and macaroni. Another breed known as rockhopper penguins nest in islands north of the Antarctic.

Penguins live in Antarctica year round, and over 50 types of flying birds spend their summer there. Some of these include albatrosses, prions, petrels, cormorants, gulls, skuas, and terns.

In Your Classroom

Have the students find the South Pole on a globe. Show how all lines of longitude meet at this point. Compare the South Pole region to the North Pole region.

Have students draw a map of Antarctica and label the South Pole, South Shetland Islands, and bodies of water around the continent. Also have them label the Transantarctic Mountains and the two land regions of West Antarctica and East Antarctica.

Plan an "Antarctic Day." If you are able to control the temperature in your classroom, keep the air cool and have students wear their coats to class. Serve cold food and beverages as a snack.

Create an "Antarctica Area" of the classroom. Have this area devoted to scientific research and discovery. Stock it with school materials and tools used in scientific study, such as a microscope or materials to use in experiments. Incorporate this Antarctic Area in your school lessons, encouraging the students to use it and share their findings with the class.

James Cook is an important explorer who was one of the first westerners to discover many different parts of the world. Have the students research his life and his travels. Assign different portions of his life or his journeys to different groups. Once each group has completed their research, have them present their knowledge to the class. Together, create a timeline of Cook's travels and hang it in the classroom for reference as you study the countries he visited.

Find pictures of Antarctica from *National Geographic* or other magazines. Cut these out and create a mural to hang on the classroom wall.

Research the locations of the various scientific research stations on Antarctica. Make a map pinpointing these places so students can picture where the scientists are living and studying.

A History of Antarctica

Long ago, ancient Greek philosophers believed a land mass covered the southern end of the earth, balancing the weight of the northern continents. The philosopher Ptolemy named this unknown land *Terra Australis Incognita*, which means "unknown southern land" in Latin. He believed the undiscovered continent was populated and fertile. But no one discovered that Antarctica really existed until much later; in fact, it was first discovered in 1820—thousands of years after the Greek philosophers' time. To honor the philosophers, the name Antarctica comes from two Greek words which in English mean "opposite the bear." This is because the Bear constellation is visible from the North Pole, which is directly opposite the South Pole.

Early Explorers

In 1772, adventurous explorer Captain James Cook set out to find the southern continent. He crossed an imaginary line known as the Arctic Circle, which is located at 66 degrees southern latitude. Cook and his crew continued on their journey for another year, but could not go much further south because huge icebergs blocked their path. Cook was never able to find land.

Because of the massive icebergs that surround Antarctica, it is difficult to determine who first spotted the continent. Many navigators journeyed to the frozen continent and explored its coastal regions, but no one began to explore the interior until the early 1900s. In 1820, three men made separate voyages to the Antarctic continent. Captain Fabian von Bellingshausen from the Russian Imperial Navy came within 20 miles of the Antarctic Peninsula. He may have spotted land, but it may have been icebergs. Captain Edward Bransfield from the British Navy made a voyage near the Shetland Islands and saw land that was most likely the Antarctic Peninsula. An American seal hunter named Nathaniel Brown Palmer also claimed to see land when he was traveling in the same area.

Early explorers

Roald Amundsen

The Antarctic Peninsula became known to some as "Graham Land" after James Graham, a leader in the British Navy during Captain Bransfield's time. Others called it Palmer Land, after the American sealer. It became universally known as the Antarctic Peninsula in 1964 when the Commonwealth Nations and the United States finally came to an agreement on the name.

Over the years, people have debated about who was the first to set foot on the continent. Some say it was an American sealer named John Davis, but others say he reached an island and not a continent. The first known landing on the continent was made by whale hunters in the 1800s.

The mysterious, isolated continent attracted many adventure-seekers. In 1911, several groups of explorers competed in a race to the South Pole. People lost their lives along the way. Norway's Roald Amundsen was the first to reach the South Pole, beating Britain's team by five weeks.

People began to explore Antarctica by air in the 1920s. By flying planes over the land, they were able to see how big the continent actually was. These air explorations piqued scientific interest in Antarctica.

The Arrival of Scientists

Scientists from all over the world were eager to study Antarctica because of its location, isolation, and unique weather and landscape. From 1957 to 1958, 12 countries participated in the International Geophysical Year (or IGY) where scientists from these various nations set up over 50 stations on the continent. They lived and researched in these stations and shared their findings with each other. The countries that participated in the IGY were Argentina, Australia, Belgium, Chile, France, Japan, New Zealand, Norway, South Africa, the Soviet Union, the United Kingdom and the United States.

Many different types of scientists joined the IGY. They researched earthquakes, gravity, magnetism, oceans, and solar activity. *Meteorologists* (scientists who study weather) studied air pressure, humidity, temperature, and wind direction. Using the information they gathered, these scientists created Antarctica's first complete weather charts. *Glaciologists* (scientists who study ice) measured thickness of the ice throughout the continent, and geologists studied the different land formations.

Antarctic Treaty

In 1959, 12 countries signed the Antarctic Treaty. This agreement ensures that no country can make claims on Antarctica. It also states that the continent will only be used for peaceful purposes such as scientific research, exploration, and tourism. Scientists who work in Antarctica must share any knowledge they gather. Military forces are not allowed to enter the continent unless they are specifically helping with scientific expeditions. No weapons or radioactive wastes are allowed on the continent because the environment must be preserved. In 1991, the 12 nations who signed the Antarctic Treaty also signed the Madrid Protocol, with states that Antarctica is a natural reserve dedicated to scientific research and peace.

Name _____   Date _____

Exploring Antarctica Timeline

Covered by a sheet of ice, Antarctica is often considered the most inaccessible place on Earth. It wasn't until the 19th century that explorers even began to travel to Antarctica to learn more about this frozen continent.

Use Internet sites or other resources to read about the exploration of Antarctica. Choose four or five key events, and briefly write them on the timeline below (in the order they occurred).

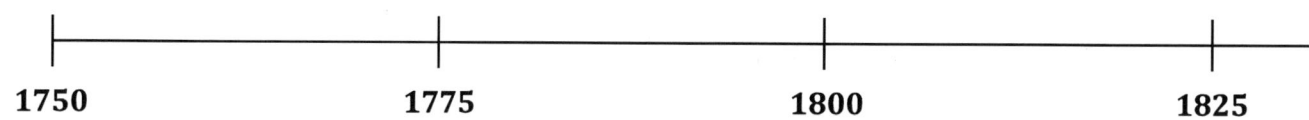

1750   1775   1800   1825

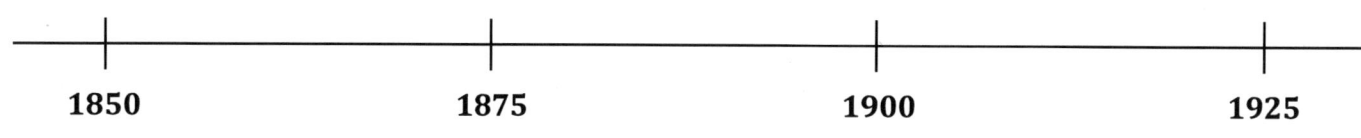

1850   1875   1900   1925

1950   1975   2000   2025

62

Antarctica - MP5124

Daily Life

Today over 40 scientific stations operate year round on Antarctica and its nearby islands. Scientists from all over the world live in these research stations, cooperating with one another and sharing their discoveries. Because of the extreme winter weather conditions, scientists can only study earthquakes, solar radiation, and weather during the winter months. Biologists come to Antarctica to observe how animals adapt to the environment.

Many scientists on Antarctica are tackling the global ozone issue. *Ozone* is an important, protective layer of gas that covers the earth. The layer above Antarctica is becoming less concentrated, so scientists there study this problem and hope to find a solution for the rest of the world. Some other ongoing issues these scientists study are climate change and interactions between the northern and southern hemispheres.

A water plant provides fresh water for the scientists, and large ships bring supplies to them and take away their waste materials and scientific samples when they leave. These ships are called *icebreakers* because they must plow through icebergs and snow on their way to deliver their goods.

Today tourism is increasing in Antarctica. The continent appeals to adventure seekers because so few people have ever been there before. The increase in tourists poses challenges to the researchers who are trying to maintain the stability of Antarctica's environment.

Answer Key

Australian English, page 13
1. i
2. o
3. a
4. g
5. n
6. m
7. b
8. j
9. h
10. c
11. k
12. d
13. l
14. e
15. f

The Night Sky, page 23
1. Crux (Southern Cross)
2. Ursa Major (Big Dipper)
3. Canis Major (Big Dog)
4. Orion (Hunter)
5. Draco (Dragon)
6. Centaurus (Centaur)

Mapping Out Papua New Guinea, page 42

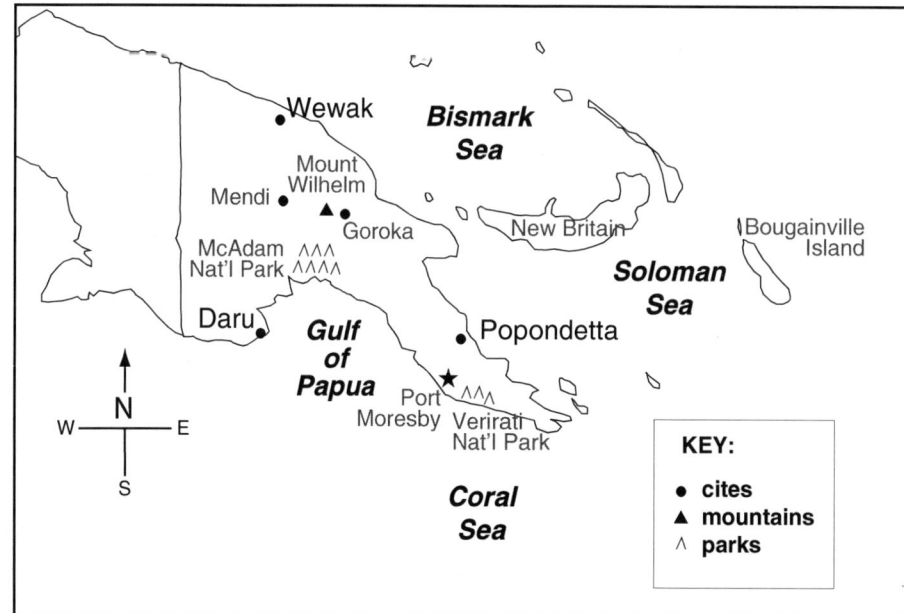

Additional Resources

Australia
Base, Graeme. *My Grandma Lived in Gooligulch*. New York: Harry N. Abrams, 1990.
Columbia World Library of Folk and Primitive Music, Volume 5. edited by Alan Lomax, Columbia Master Works.
Fox, Mem. *Possum Magic*. New York: Voyager Books, 1991.
Fox, Mem. *Koala Lou*. New York: Voyager Books, 1994.
Grant J., ed. *The Australopedia*. Fitzroy, Australia: McPhee Gribble/ Penguin Books, 1988.
Lindsay, Norman. *The Magic Pudding, The Adventures of Bunyip Bluegum*. New York: New York Review Books, 2004.
Mountford, Charles P. *The Dawn of Time: Australian Aboriginal Myths*. Adelaide, Australia: Rigby Ltd., 1989.
Vaughan, Marcia K. *Wombat Stew*. Illustrated by Pamela Lofts. Melbourne: Ashton Scholastic Pty. Ltd., 2001.

New Zealand
Landau, Elaine. *Australia and New Zealand*. New York: Scholastic, 2000.
Smelt, Roselynn. *Cultures of the World: New Zealand*. New York: Benchmark Books, 2009.
Theunissen, Steve. *The Maori of New Zealand*. Minneapolis: Lerner Publishing Group, 2002.

Papua New Guinea
Gascoigne, Ingrid. *Cultures of the World: Papua New Guinea*. New York: Benchmark Books, 2009.
Margolies, Barbara A. *Warriors, Wigmen, and the Crocodile People: Journeys in Papua New Guinea*. New York: Simon & Schuster, 1993.

Fiji
Ball, John. *Let's Visit Fiji*. London: Burke Publishing Company, 1985.
Ngcheog-lum, Roseline. *Cultures of the World: Fiji*. New York: Benchmark Books, 2010.

Antarctica
Friedman, Mel. *Antarctica*. New York: Scholastic, 2009.
Kalman, Bobbie. *Explore Antarctica*. New York: Crabtree Publishing Company, 2007.
Osborne, Mary Pope. *Magic Tree House Research Guide: Penguins and Antarctica*. New York: Random House, 2008.

Notes